THE HISTORY
OF
THE 107 REGIMENT
ROYAL ARMOURED CORPS
(KINGS OWN)

JUNE 1940 — FEBRUARY 1946

The Naval & Military Press Ltd

Published by

The Naval & Military Press Ltd
Unit 5 Riverside, Brambleside
Bellbrook Industrial Estate
Uckfield, East Sussex
TN22 1QQ England

Tel: +44 (0)1825 749494

www.naval-military-press.com
www.nmarchive.com

In reprinting in facsimile from the original, any imperfections are inevitably reproduced and the quality may fall short of modern type and cartographic standards.

CONTENTS

Section I —	Formation and Training	5
Section II —	Operations up to FALAISE	9
Section III —	LE HAVRE and CLARKEFORCE	13
Section IV —	Operations up to the RHINE	18
Section V —	Conclusion	22

Appendix A —	Casualties	24
Appendix B —	Report on Raid on ESQUAY, 2. Aug 44	27
Appendix C —	Reports from 'B' Squadron on Minor Actions from 16—18 Aug 44	31
Appendix D —	Report of the attack on LE HAVRE	34
Appendix E —	Report on Raid in ST OEDENRODE AREA (from 'C' Squadron)	36
Appendix F —	Immediate report to 34 Tank Bde — Operations with CLARKEFORCE, 20—29 Oct 44	37
Appendix G —	Report of action in capture of BLERICK	50
Appendix H —	Immediate report to 34 Armd Bde on actions with 51 (H) Division from 8—28 Feb 45	53
Appendix I —	Honours and Awards — Citations	75

REGIMENTAL HISTORY
SECTION I — FORMATION AND TRAINING

In January 1940 a number of Holding Battalions were formed to take the flow of trained men from the Infantry Training Centres and hold them until they were required by the service battalions. The King's Own Company of the 7th Holding Battalion was formed at DENBIGH, in N. WALES, and later moved to RHYL. Three of its platoon commanders were regular Officers of the "King's Own" — 2/Lts. J. H. Waters Taylor, D. H. Davies, and G. I. Thwaites — who were later to become Squadron Leaders in the 107 RAC. In may 1940 further expansion took place, and the 50th (Holding) Battalion of the King's Own Royal Regiment was formed at HEYSHAM in Lancashire; the King's Own Company at RHYL was disbanded, and its officers and men joined the 50th.

The Commanding Officer of the 50th was Lt-Col S. H. Crow, who had been up till then Second-in-Command of the King's Own I. T. C.

It now became obvious that the title of the Battalion was a misnomer; it acted first as a reception and refitting centre for men of the B. E. F. (from DUNKIRK), and then the Battalion received direct from civil life some seven to eight hundred men, and embarked on a course of elementary training which had up till then been the concern of the Infantry Training Centres. Company detachements were formed at BORWICK and HALTON MILL based a few miles North of LANCASTER.

Almost before Company training was under way, the unit became a service battalion, the 10th King's Own, and was brigaded with battalions of the King's Regiment and the Border Regiment (the 12th and 9th) into the 225th (Independent) Infantry Brigade. This took place in October 1940. Throughout November and December more intensive training took place and in January 1941 the battalion, as part of the Brigade moved across North England and took over responsibility for the defence of a stretch of the Northumbrian coast from the small fishing harbour of CRASTER, north to almost BAMBURG CASTLE.

The responsibility for the entire Northumberland coast belonged to a static formation — The Northumberland Division — which 225 Brigade joined. A period of intensive work began in some of the worst weather of the war. Platoon and Company localities were sited to cover some 14 miles of coast by small arms fire, positions were dug, wired and mined. The entire coast line was wired and patrolled day and night. Nevertheless time had to be found for Battalion training, and for the Summer the Brigade was relieved by one from the 59th Division and the Battalion moved to HAYDEN BRIDGE where it did Battalion and higher training as part of 59 Division, returning to the beaches in September. In November the news came that the Northumberland Division was to break up. In 225 Brigade the 9th Border Regiment remained Infantry and were to serve with the Indian Army; the 12th King's Regiment were to become gunners, and the 10th King's Own Royal Regiment was to convert to a heavy tank battalion of the R. A. C. The Battalion was relieved of coastal defence by a unit of the 15th (Scottish) Division, and the work of conversion began. It moved back again into the TYNE VALLEY (Nov. 1941) and was brigaded with two other infantry battalions into the 35th Army Tank Brigade. Regimental HQ was at PRUDHOE.

On January 1st 1942, the title of the Regiment was changed to the 151st Regiment, R. A. C. Several Officers and men remained as infantry and were posted to infantry or reconnaissance units; their places were taken by specialists from The Royal Tank Regiment. The main work of conversion was done by means of War Office Courses; all Officers in turn were sent oither to general courses at SANDHURST or to special courses at LULWORTH, and nearly all the men attended similar courses at various depots. The Regimental strength in the Station was reduced to about six officers and one hundred men. The first tank arrived in February 1942 — a Churchill 2 pounder — and was collected from the station by the Technical Adjutant. It entered the village broadside on, sliding sideways downhill along the icy street, coming to rest in its tank park, and there, since it developed its usual share of the Churchill's early mechanical troubles, it spent most of its time But more tanks arrived, and men returned from courses until troop and even squadron training could begin. A troop at first consisted of one Churchill and two carriers, but gradually as more tanks arrived it began to wear a more orthodox appearance. In August the Regiment changed Brigades, replacing the 11th Bn R. T. R. (a Matilda Unit) in the 25th Tank Brigade, and moved to WESTGATE, in Kent. This Brigade was part of 43rd (Wessex) Division, an experimental heavy division, consisting of two brigades of infantry and one of tanks. In September, 34 Tank Brigade replaced the 25 Brigade in 43 Division, and the 151 R. A. C. changed over to the new Brigade replacing the North Irish Horse. 34 Tank Brigade headquarters and two of its regiments — 147 and 153 R. A. C. — were at WORTHING. The 151st remained at WESTGATE, and in October undertook its first regimental scheme. Returning from this exercise the column was attacked by enemy aircraft outside CANTERBURY and one man was killed and one wounded. In the latter part of October the Regiment moved to MINEHEAD in Somerset, and fired its first Battle Practice. From there it moved to WORTHING to join the rest of the Brigade, and more Squadron and Regimental training took place on the Downs just north of the town with units of the infantry brigades in the Division. The Regiment was back in WESTGATE in December, as the whole brigade moved over into Kent, and was visited by General Borrett, the Colonel of the King's Own Royal Regiment.

In January 1943, it was obvious that changes of the first order were afoot. Lt.-Col. Crow was due to relinquish command in the following April, and his successor, Major H. H. K. Rowe, of the Royal Tank Regiment, now joined the Regiment as Second-in-Command. At this time too, the Regiment began to make full use of a first class tank training area, the country around STONE STREET, the Roman road which runs almost due SOUTH from CANTERBURY. The GHQ exercise 'SPARTAN' filled the latter part of February and early March, and on the 4th April Lt.-Col. H. H. K. Rowe assumed command of the Regiment.

In May the Regiment changed quarters, moving out to live on the training area; Regimental Headquarters moved to GORSLEY, a country house a mile or so from the village of BRIDGE, on the Canterbury—Dover road. A period of most intensive training now began; Troop and Squadron training, interspersed with Regimental schemes and full scale Divisional exercise. In June tanks and tank crews went north to KIRKCUDBRIGHT, to fire Battle Practices, and this was followed almost immediately by another GHQ exercise 'HARLEQUIN' in which the machinery for breaking up units into invasion craft loads and moving them to points of embarkation was rehearsed. The Regiment was away from GORSLEY for about four weeks in all, to the middle of September, mainly spent at OTTERDEN, near MAIDSTONE. Shortly after the return to GORSLEY, a second period of Field Firing was arranged, this time at WARCOP, in WESTMORLAND- where tanks and crews arrived in October. Meanwhile the transport Echelon moved to winter quarters at FOLKESTONE, where they were later joined by the tanks.

At this time 34 Tank Brigade left the 43 Division which took in a third infantry Brigade, reverting to the normal constitution of an infantry division. The Brigade became 'Army Troops' and was attached to 12 Corps. Training began now in co-operation with other divisions of the Corps, and particularly with the 59th Division, with which the Brigade worked in November on a Corps exercise — 'CANUTE'.

At the beginning of 1944, the title of the Regiment was changed to 107th Regiment, R. A. C. (King's Own). Some time before the 10th King's Own had been converted to 151 R. A. C., the 5th Bn of the King's Own, a pre-war Territorial battalion had been converted, and, as 107 R. A. C., had formed part of an armoured division. In December 1943 this Regiment was disbanded, and the 151st assumed its identity.

Part of the Regiment in January moved to the South Downs-quarters were in SOUTHWICK, a suburb of BRIGHTON, for further training with 214 Brigade the new Infantry Brigade of 43 Division, and a few weeks later the whole regiment moved to GOODNESTONE, a few miles north of FOLKESTONE.

In April, Lt.—Col. Rowe was posted away from the Regiment to assume the appointment of GSO. I, 79 Armoured Division, and the Second-in-Command, Major S. H. P. K. Greenway, temporarily assumed Command, to take the Regiment for another short period to the South Downs, and then in May, to move it to its concentration area at HEADLEY, in Surrey. The new Commanding Officer, Lt.-Col. D. H. Courtenay, of the Royal Tank Regiment, arrived shortly afterwards. The waterproofing of all vehicles, and wading tests, were the main occupations of the Regiment at this time. Ten days after D-day (6. June 1944) the Regiment split up into three craft loads, and moved to transit camps RHQ at LEE-ON-SOLENT, and the other two in the outskirts of PORTSMOUTH. Advance parties had left for NORMANDY a few days previously. The Regiment spent about two weeks in the transit camps und did not embark the first craft load until early morning of June 30th 1944. The remainder of the Regiment embarked the following day. Disembarkation on the beach at COURSEULLES took place on July 1st and 2nd and by the 3 rd the Regiment was concentrated at CULLY except for a small rear party left at HEADLEY.

SECTION II — OPERATIONS UP TO FALAISE.

It is relevant here to note briefly the composition of the Regiment. The 2 pounder had long ago given place to the 6 pounder and the 75 mm as the main tank armament, and the 3 inch howitzer had been replaced by a 95 mm Short barrelled howitzer for close support. The reconnaissance troop, which for a long time had used carriers, was now equipped with a light American tank, the Stuart.

Lt.-Col. Courtenay, commanding the Regiment, had as his Second-in-Command, Major S. H. P. K. Greenway of the Royal Tank Regiment; the Squadron Leaders were, Majors J. H. Curtis (HQ Sqn) A. Biddell (posted from 7 Armoured Division) ('A' Squadron), D. H. Davies ('B' Squadron) and J. A. Waters Taylor ('C' Squadron).

The Regiment stayed at Cully for almost a fortnight, broken only by a march across BASLY, north of CAEN, during the attack on this town; there was no task however, and the Regiment moved back to harbour. It went into action for the first time in the evening of Saturday July 15th, with a battalion of the 15th (Scottish) Division, the 2nd Glasgow Highlanders. The infantry intention, with the support of 107 R. A. C. and one troop of flame throwing tanks, was to capture a small hamlet, BON REPOS, and the village ESQUAY. During the night July 14/15. the Regiment moved forward to an assembly area at MOUEN. on the BAYEUX—CAEN railway line; and crossed the river ODON to form up on the reverse slopes of Hill 112 in the evening of July 15th. The attack began at 2145 hours, with 'A' and 'B' Squadrons supporting the infantry 'C' Suadron in reserve. Visibility was poor owing to excessive use of smoke, and the tanks had to move on to the final objectives with the infantry in order to support them; no enemy tanks were encountered but in the early stages there was trouble from anti-tank guns, and Lieutenant Turner, commander of 8 Troop of 'B' Squadron, was killed when his tank was hit by an 88 mm, which was immediately afterwards destroyed by the remaining tanks of his troop. Darknees fell whilst the forward tank troops were still in the orchards and houses of BON REPOS AND ESQUAY, and these troops had some difficulty in navigating back to the forward rally. There were no searchlights to give the artificial movement light which was found so invaluable in later actions. The forward rally was in the same area as the forming up place and the Regiment had to remain there until first light. Both before and after the attack the enemy shelled this area with medium and heavy artillery.

The task of 'C' Squadron in reserve had been to tow forward 17 pounder Anti-tank guns on to the newly won positions, which involved crossing one of our own minefields; their guides however never arrived at the Rendezvous and this project was abandoned. At first light the Regiment rear-rallied at MOUEN. This attack was intended to be the prelude to a larger scale advance to secure the high ground which dominated BON REPOS and ESQUAY; this advance did not materialise, and, the two villages being therefore untenable, the Glasgow Highlanders withdrew. A day later the Regiment again advanced over the ODON and took up positions just in rear of our forward Infantry localities at the hamlet of TOURMAUVILLE in the sector held by 53 (Welsh) Division, and remained there for ten days during which it supported infantry raids, one on a Battalion scale, on the enemy lines at BON REPOS and EVRECY. At this time the transport Echelon was bombed by the German Air Force and received several casualties. When relieved, the Regiment moved back to MARCELET by night, and the folowing day to CRISTOT for a rest of 48 hours, then again into the line in the region of TOURMAUVILLE for another week, but this time on a wider front, as 53 Division had taken over the front of 43 Division (including the 112 feature) in addition to its own. Several raids in force were undertaken mainly to ensure that certain armoured formations of the enemy were still facing the division.

This was by now almost the only static part of the front; the Americans had broken right out of the CHERBOURG peninsula, and a limited breakout had been achieved on the right flank of the British Army. To this, in the region of VILLERS BOCAGE, the Regiment was Suddenly switched, and put under command of 176 Brigade of the 59 th Division for a pursuit march to the River ORNE, which was in two days reached at a point opposite GRIMBOSQ. The river at this part was fordable at almost any point, but the approaches on the West bank were steep and unsuitable for tanks, and a railway embankment on the far side was an additional obstacle.

The three battalions of infantry (the 7 Norfolk Regiment 1/7 South Staffordshire Regiment, and 1/6 North Staffordshire Regiment), started to cross the river at 2200 hrs on 6th August and by shortly after midnight a bridgehead had been established without any great difficulty approximately a mile deep and two miles wide, centreing on the cross roads at the hamlet of BRIEUX, up to which led the road from a destroyed bridge over the river. 'A' Squadron with the help of a section of A. V. R. E. s (Assault Churchills manned by Royal Engineers), crossed the river at 0900 hrs 7th August followed by 'C' Squadron. Both Squadrons joined their infantry; 'B' Squadron had a separate task, lining the west bank of the river further up stream, in a possible anti-tank role. Throughout the day the bridgehead was heavily mortared by the enemy from the FORET de GRIMBOSQ, and there was also evidence that there was enemy armour concealed in the wood. It was decided to extend the bridgehead to the South and 'A' Squadron, with the battalion of infantry holding the Southern sector, lined up at 1900 hrs to do this. 'C' Squadron's dispositions had been altered in the afternoon, and at this particular time communications within the Squadron were not at their best. A few minutes after 1900 hrs, the enemy launched a counter attack by infantry supported by heavy tanks debouching from the wood along the whole length of the bridgehead. The Norfolks' positions were over-run but small groups of men continued to fight; one Officer of the Norfolks was awarded the Victoria Cross for his gallantry in commanding such a group which was almost surrounded, and the Commander of the one tank which could support him, Sjt Brooker of 'C' Squadron was awarded the Military Medal; this tank destroyed two Panthers. 'C' Squadron HQ Troop was cut off and the Reconnaissance Officer, Capt. Parker, was killed by an A. P. shot which penetrated his tank. 'A' Squadron was caught out of 'Hull Down' positions since it was forming up to attack, and suffered heavy tank casualties as a result. Darkness was now falling, and as the enemy tanks lost their mobility, our own infantry stood firm. Small battle groups of infantry with anti-tank guns were organised to prevent the enemy crossing the river. In this they were successful, but they were unable to prevent him from mining the road from the river crossing leading to the BRIEUX crossroads. This road, at this time, was the only exit from the river and was almost a tank defile. 'B' Squadron was ordered to cross at first light the following day 8th August to restore the situation, and it did an approach march during the night up to the crossing. At first light Major Davies led across, after having spent several hours reconnoitring the bridgehead on foot, and planning with the infantry commanders. The mined sunken road delayed him for some time; he and his Squadron

Reconnaissance Officer, Captain Cockroft, cleared the minefield, whilst damaged tanks were being pulled to one side. When he was eventually past this obstacle, his own tank was destroyed by enemy A. P. The Squadron was so reduced in strength by this time that it was unable to do more than hold a small inner perimeter round the exit for the river crossing.

About midday the enemy launched another counter-attack. This was beaten off by a composite half squadron made up of remnants of 'A' and 'C' Squadrons organised and commanded with great vigour and gallantry by Capt. Caton, Reconnaissance Officer of 'A' Squadron. By skilful use of what little ground cover there was, and by accurate and timely calls from a regiment of medium artillery which was in support, the enemy Tiger tanks were driven off. In the evening the bridgehead was comparatively firm again and the Regiment was relieved by another Regiment of the Brigade, 147 R. A. C. and withdrew to rear rally. Major Davies, who was originally recommended for the D. S. O., Capt. Cockroft and Capt. Caton, were awarded the Military Cross for their part in the battle, in which the Regiment suffered severe casuasties to Officers, men and tanks; recovery of tanks went on throughout the battle, but the following day the Regiment could only muster a squadron strength of tanks.

On 9th August, this composite squadron, commanded by Major Davies, crossed the ORNE, and supporting successively 177 and 197 Brigades of 59 Division, advanced to cut the road from FLERS to FALAISE. This squadron advanced, fighting many small actions, for 8—10 days, but was not released until the infantry were astride the road South West of FALAISE.

On 14th August, Lt.-Col. H. H. K. Rowe, R. T. R., was posted back to the Regiment and re-assumed command on that date, having been been on staff duties with 79 Armoured Division for four months.

The Regiment now concentrated West of FALAISE for reorganisation.

SECTION III — LE HAVRE AND CLARKEFORCE

The last week of August and the first of September were spent in this harbour in re-organisation.

The 153rd Regiment, R. A. C., of 34 Tank Brigade had been disbanded, and now an entire squadron of this Regiment, commanded by Major E. C. Garner, joined 107 R. A. C. forming its 'C' Squadron. Major Thwaites, who had left 107 at TOUR-MAUVILLE to command a squadron of 153, rejoined to command 'A' Squadron. Major Biddell took over command of 'HQ' Squadron. After the re-organisation of the Regiment, the remaining time was spent in training.

From FALAISE the Regiment moved on its tracks over the SEINE through ROUEN to ANGERVILLE L'ORCHER, a few miles East of LE HAVRE, then invested by 1 Corps; it was placed in support of 147 Infantry Brigade of 49 Infantry Division, with the task in the general assault on the port, of capturing the high ground on the Eastern outskirts of the town. The Corps attack on a two divisional front, began on the evening of September 10th but the Regiment was not employed until the evening of the following day. In moving forward delay was caused on the 147 Infantry Brigade front at the outset by minefields on all tracks and roads, but after a slow start the attack gathered momentum; the enemy who had been subjected to heavy bombing and artillery bombardments, offered comparatively light resistance, and the high ground was cleared by evening. The infantry began to clear the outer suburbs which were their final objective, and the Regiment harboured for the night North of the town. On the following day only mopping up remained to be done (in one case of a pill box to which the enemy had returned during the night), and shortly after mid-day 12 September, the Regiment was re-released by the infantry brigade commander.

From its rear rally the Regiment moved back to ANGERVILLE thence to BOSC-LE-HARD,, where it was grounded for two weeks, as the speed of the Army Group advance carried our forces through FRANCE and BELGIUM, and all transport was sent away to serve with the R. A. S. C. as supply columns. As the front became established however, it became obvious that there would now be tasks again for Churchills, and the

Regiment began its week's march into HOLLAND, on tracks as for as the BELGIAN Frontier, then on transporters through BRUSSELS to the ALBERT CANAL, and again on tracks through EINDHOVEN to ST. OEDENRODE. Here, in support of 158 Brigade, 53 (Welsh) Division, which was under command of the 51st Highland Division, it held part of the Western flank of the famous corridor which extended up to ARNHEM. The Regiment was called upon to assist in raids with a troop or squadron, and only once "stood to", to deal with a threatened counter-attack. This corridor had previously been cut by the enemy at about this point but it soon became clear that the danger from this was now largely past, and at the end of a week, the Regiment moved through EINDHOVEN and TURNHOUT to GIERLE, a village just south of the ANTWERP—TURNHOUT CANAL, where planning for a new operation commenced.

34 Tank Brigade now came under command of 49 Division, whose general task was an offensive towards TILBURG, in conjunction with the remainder of Troops under command Canadian Army in their advance North to the River MAAS. When the enemy's line North of the ANTWERP—TURNHOUT CANAL had been broken, an armoured force was to pass through and exploit. This force — CLARKEFORCE — was commanded by Brigadier W. S. Clarke, the Commander of 34 Tank Brigade and consisted of 49 Division Reconnaissance Regiment, 107 R. A. C. a troop of self propelled anti tank guns (17 pounder) and a company of infantry (from the Leicestershire Regiment). The anti-tank guns and infantry, which were to be carried on a squadron of tanks, were placed under command of 107 R. A. C.

At 0600 hrs on October 20th the Regimental Group concentrated at ST LEONARD and was launched at 1600 hrs through the STAPELHEIDE area, captured that day; its objective was WUESTWEZEL, but it had first to gain a crossing over a stream West of LOENHOUT. The bridge — known as STONE BRIDGE — was known to be standing, and at 1630 hrs it was captured and crossed by the Reconnaissance Troop of the Regiment, followed by 'B' Squadron 'A' Squadron passed over next to expand the bridgehead, then 'C' Squadron carrying the infantry, who in the failing light moved on to WUESTWEZEL and captured that village, only light opposition being met in the town and this was quickly cleared of the surprised enemy. 'A' Squadron of the Reconnaissance Regiment with two troops of tanks was then left to guard the bridge, and the Regiment moved into WUESTWEZEL in darkness. At 2300 hrs the advance up the main road to NIEUWMOER was begun, the Regiment's troop of light tanks, commanded by Lieut. Hogan again leading. The night was extremely dark so that the advance had to be led on foot and progress was slow. Some resistance was met from snipers and enemy with bazookas, and in one place a road block was encountered, so that it was not until 0300 hrs that the Regiment harboured approximately a mile and a half North West of WUESTWEZEL. At 0800 hrs the advance to NIEUWMOER was resumed a squadron of the Reconnaissance Regiment moving ahead of 107 R. A. C. and the positions gained being taken over by a 'follow up' infantry battalion in support. This advance was slowed by a blown bridge and a tank obstacle, and by fire from enemy self propelled guns from the village itself. 'A' Squadron was ordered to move round to the West and then North of the village, to cut the northern exits from it; in doing so it lost one tank, its gunner was killed and its commander Lieut. Mitchell and two others of its crew were severely wounded, and it caught fire. In spite of the fact that the whole area was under small arms fire, the driver, Lance Corporal Piper, pulled all the wounded clear of the tank to safety in a nearby ditch. For this action he was awarded the D. C. M. As soon as 'A' Squadron were round the village, 'C' Squadron and their Company of Infantry were launched from the southwest to clear the village. Whilst this was proceeding the Reconnaissance Troop was ordered to follow 'A Squadron and contact them north of the village, thereafter to remain halted keeping a large wood to the North of the village under observation. Unfortunately, the troop went too far North in an excess of enthusiasm, and ran into a nest of enemy S. Ps and infantry in the large wood. The Reconnaissance Troop lost four tanks, three men were killed, three more were wounded, and one was taken prisoner. NIEUWMOER was cleared soon afterwards and the Regiment harboured for the night in that village. The next day the advance was resumed North towards ESSCHEN and enemy infantry and S. Ps were successfully engaged, the Regiment remaining in defensive positions in the area South of SCHRIEK until infantry could arrive to take over. During this day part of the transport Echelon, commanded by RSM Greig, was ambushed in a wood south of NIEUWMOER. This wood had not been completely cleared, and, in fact a large number of Germans, commanded by a resolute Officer who would not allow them to surrender, were hiding in it. The harbour party of an Artillery Brigade Headquarters was also captured and this party of 107 R. A. C. RSM Greig, attempting to get away and give the alarm, was shot. The remainder were freed next day as the Germans had left over night. On the following day, October 23rd, the **Regiment rallied back to NIEUWMOER and** plans were made for an attack on rising ground running East and West through SCHRIEK, which took place on the 24th and was successful. As soon as the infantry (a battalion of the Duke of Wellington's Regiment) were firmly established, the Regiment withdrew to the village of ACHTERBROEK, where it passed a day and two nights in planning the next phase of the advance.

At 0600 hrs, October 26th, the Regiment concentrated at ESSCHEN on the Dutch Frontier, and at 1000 hrs was launched through the area of NISPEN, captured the previous night. It harboured for the night in the area of BREMBOSCH, where the fiercest opposition was encountered. Three tanks of 'C' Squadron were put out of action (including the Squadron Leaders) and Major Davies, commander 'B' Squadron, was severely wounded together with two members of his crew. The next day October 27th, was probably the most difficult of the entire advance. Between BREMBOSCH and WOUWSCHE HIL there was an artificial anti-tank ditch and the road was closed by a concrete block. At 0800 hrs the Leicesters, now reinforced by two companys, supported by fire from the tanks, crossed the obstacles by means of ladders, under enemy small arms fire. A bulldozer then attempted to pile up enough rubble against the obstacles to form a ramp but this did not succeed. Accordingly A. P. and H. E. fire from a Troop of tanks and 17 pounder S.Ps was directed at the top of the concrete and approximately 3 feet of the to was knocked off which enabled the tanks to climb over; all this time there was constant fire from enemy positions in the surrounding fields, and Captain McKenna, the Reconnaissance Officer, of 'B' Squadron, was killed by small arms fire whilst reconnoitering on foot. At 1100 hrs the obstacle was crossed, and the Regiment advanced to WOUWSCHE HIL where under successive strong enemy medium concentrations, a plan was made to capture OOSTLAAR, the next village North. Here also direct contact was made with the leading troops of the Canadian armour advancing to BERGEN—OP—ZOOM on the Regiment's left flank. It was known that S. Ps were guarding the direct approach to OOSTLAAR and it was decided to capture the village by a right flanking movement through the hamlet of HAINK, which a Squadron of the Reconnaissance Regiment reported clear. The Regiment was engaged by enemy S. Ps on the way to HAINK and one tank was knocked out; by using smoke the cover of the buildings was reached, but the enemy brought down strong concentrations of mediums on to the area and also engaged our tanks with 75 mm and 88 S. Ps. A plan was made to cross the open country to OOSTLAAR but this move was delayed owing to a number of small mishaps. Several tanks bogged on the very bad ground or slipped tracks, and the Commanding Officer held up the advance until all tanks were ready to move. Just before moving off enemy S. Ps opened fire and destroyed one tank; the S. Ps were engaged and one was destroyed. About half an hour was spent in towing bogged tanks clear and righting others, and during this time the Regiment was shelled and fired upon by A. P. continuously. Eventually the Regiment moved out of HAINK one up, and advanced to OOSTLAAR under cover of smoke screens on either flank, passing through one of the heaviest concentrations of enemy medium artillery that had been experienced. OOSTLAAR was reached as darkness was falling and pre-arranged positions were taken up.

The village could not be completely cleared that night and at first light on October 28th an enemy S. P. opened fire on 'C' Squadron, put one tank out of action and destroyed three vehicles of the supply train wchich had just replenished the Squadron. Shortly after 0800 hrs an attack was put in against WOUW, the Regiment consisting now of 'A' Squadron and a depleted 'C' Squadron, supporting 11th Battalion of the Royal Scots Fusiliers. The town was attacked by a left flanking movement which first cut the road to BERGEN—OP—ZOOM, and then entered the town. Enemy S. Ps withdrew to the outskirts and the town was for some time under severe H. E. and A. P. fire until the infantry, supported by 'A' Squadron, finished clearing the town and the S. Ps were driven back by concentrated artillery fire. The Regiment harboured for the night in WOUW and the next day supported by fire a successfull attack by the 9th Royal Tank Regiment to clear the right flank up to ROOSENDAAL. Units of CLARKEFORCE having carried out their tasks were then reverted to their normal commands, and the Regiment remained at WOUW for rest and refitting.

In ten days of continual fighting it had advanced approximately twenty five miles over flat Dutch territory against the enemy rearguard screen of S. Ps and infantry strong points; it had destroyed 8 S. Ps and taken 230 prisoners; its own losses in officers and men were 9 killed and 32 wounded, and one man captured; it had 19 tanks put out of action, but of these only two Churchills and four Stuarts were completely destroyed. Major Garner, the Commander of 'C' Squadron was awarded the Military Cross for his conspicuous gallantry throughout all these actions.

SECTION IV — OPERATIONS UP TO THE RHINE

CLARKEFORCE ended on October 29th, and the Regiment was not in action again until December 3rd. The intervening time was spent at WOUW, BREDA, OUDENBOSCH and BUDEL. From BUDEL the Regiment, less 'A' Squadron concentrated at MAASBREE, preparatory to the capture of BLERICK, a suburb of VENLO West of the MAAS. The town was surrounded by an anti tank ditch covered on both sides by extensive minefields. The plan was that armour of the 79th Armoured Division (22 Dragoons) should flail lanes through the minefields and bridge the anti tank obstacle with A.V.R.Es; four battalions of the infantry of 15th Scottish Division were then to go through the gaps in armoured infantry carriers (Kangaroos), and, supported by flame throwers complete the capture of the town up to the MAAS; two Squadrons of 107 R.A.C. were to support the operation by fire from the nearside of the anti tank ditch. All went well except on the left sector where the going was so bad that 'B' Squadron had to spend some time towing bogged flail tanks. Without this assistance the Flails would not have got into action in this sector. The only opposition was from the enemy artillery concentrating on the area of the Forming Up Points and of the anti tank ditch, and 'B' Squadron Leader was severely wounded in the face early in the operation. The armoured part of the operation was almost over by 1400 hrs and by this time two battalions of the infantry were up to the MAAS, and on the left one battalion was half way into BLERICK. Tanks were therefore withdrawn except for two troops of 'B' Squadron which remained to support the fourth battalion of infantry in its attack on the factory area in the Northern part of the town. This was completed by mid afternoon and all tanks rear rallied at MAASBREE to march from there to NEDEWEERT. During this move which took place in darkness, Capt. Julius, the Reconnaissance Officer of 'B' Squadron, was killed when his tank overturned in falling down an embankment along which the road ran. This was the only fatal Regimental casualty of the operation.

At NEDERWEERT, Capt. P. E. Tapson, who up to this time had been Adjutant of the Regiment, since its re-organisation in FRANCE, assumed command of 'B' Squadron.

The Regiment then moved to join the rest of the Brigade at BRUNSSUM, where under the 43rd Division, it was to put in an attack up to the main SIEGFRIED LINE defences in the region east of SITTARD, on the GERMAN — DUTCH frontier. This attack had to be postponed owing to ground conditions which were so bad that two or three days hard frost were necessary to permit tank movement. The Regiment left BRUNSSUM on transporters for TILBURG, for training with 43rd Division, prior to the turning of the SIEGFRIED LINE in the REICHSWALD AREA, but the destination was changed en route owing to the Hun breakthrough in the ARDENNES, and it concentrated eventually at TONGRES. At TONGRES, time was spent planning counter attacks with 129 Brigade of 43 Division, in the event of the enemy capturing LIEGE or crossing the River MEUSE. The regiment remained here for about a fortnight, which covered the Christmas period. Just before the Regiment left TONGRES it came under command of 5 Guards Armoured Brigade of the Guards Armoured Division. When the German drive through the ARDENNES appeared to be checked, the Regiment was moved SOUTH to the area of DINANT, and were in support of 5 Para Brigade of 6 Airborne Division who had been sent out from England at 48 hours notice. The Regiment took up positions on the East of the River MEUSE in the area of CELLES, the village which marked the deepest penetration of the enemy's counter offensive and from which he had been driven a few days previously. The undoubted scenic beauties of the ARDENNES were little compensation for the extreme discomfort and danger of tank movement in hilly country under such conditions. At CELLES the Regiment remained for a week, before moving to CHEVETOGNE and supporting the other two brigades (6 Airlanding and 3 Para Brigades) of the Division. As the Allied counterattacks started, the Regiment went into 30 Corps Reserve and tied up with 153 Brigade (51 Highland Division) who were under command of 53 Welsh Division. This involved a move to JENEFFE, a few miles away from CHEVETOGNE, which would under normal conditions have been a day's march, but which in actual fact took three days to complete. 53 Welsh Division were relieved by 51 Highland Division and the Regiment reverted to command of 34 Tank Brigade.

A long march back into HOLLAND then began, first to NAMUR on tracks, then by transporters to EINDHOVEN, and again by tracks to OIRSCHOT, a small village a mile or so East of BOXTEL, on the EINDHOVEN — s' HERTOGENBOSH road, where planning for the delayed attack on the Northern end of the SIEGFRIED LINE began. The Regiment now came under command of the 51 Highland Division and concentrated on February 6th 1945, in a large wood West of the REICHSWALD. The attack began at 1030 hrs on February 8th after a five hour hours artillery bombardment, and in spite of thickly sewn mines and extremely difficult ground (the mud was so deep that movement was only possible along a few tracks). The two infantry brigades supported by 'A' und 'B' Squadrons secured the high ground in the Western Corner of the REICHSWALD their objective for the first day. During this the going was so difficult that many tanks bogged; on the other hand it was vital that what few tracks were available should be kept clear of tanks and the work of recovery crews was here more impotant than ever. The Recovery Serjeant of 'B' Squadron was wounded by a mine and his place was taken by the Mechanist Sjt. of 'B' Squadron, Sjt. Maclean, who for his work in recovering under small arms fire, a flail tank and a Churchill with its track off, which were blocking the main axis of advance, was awarded the Military Medal.

At first light the following day the third infantry brigade supported by 'C' Squadron passed through and began to advance along the southern edge of the forest, and 'A' Squadron resumed its advance through the wood further to the North; meanwhile 'B' Squadron wheeled first West to link up with the Canadians in the former front line South-East of MOOK, and then South to the main road MOOK-GENNEP. Now that this road could be used, the advance on this sector was more rapid, and on February 10th the 5/7th Gordons of 153 Brigade, supported by 'B' Squadron, captured OTTERSUM and grained a small bridgehead over the river NIERS at GENNEP. In the centre and left hand sectors (152 Brigade and 'C' Squadron, and 154 Brigade and 'A' Squadron) progess was still slow owing to the appalling ground conditions, and the fierce resistance of the enemy. During the night a Bailey bridge was built under shell and machine gun fire over the River NIERS, and on February 11th 'B' Squadron passed over and supported the final clearance of GENNEP. Owing to the fact 152 Brigade were tired after hard fighting through the REICHSWALD, 154 Brigade supported by 'A' Squadron passed through the former brigade that evening and captured the village of HEKKENS and pushed on South to NERGENA. The following day 153 Brigade ('B' Squadron) extended their positions to the South and South-East; an enemy counter attack supported by tanks on February 13th on these positions was beaten off, Lieut. Walker the Troop Leader supporting the 5/7 Gordons, who were being attacked, was killed by H. E. fire from an enemy tank whilst out of his own tank on reconnaissance. Meanwhile 154 Brigade ('A' Squadron) closed up to the River NIERS South of HEKKENS and crossed during the night supported by tank fire; 'A' Squadron followed the next day, using the bridge at GENNEP, and joined its infantry in the area of VILLER. KESSEL was captured the same day (February 15th). On February 18th 'C' Squadron crossed the River NIERS (again at GENNEP) and moved to a concentration area. Its infantry that night attacked the outer defences of GOCH, and at first light 'C' Squadron moved forward to assist in the reduction of pillboxes bypassed by the leading infantry. 153 Brigade now passed through and, supported by 'B' Squadron, captured the Western half of GOCH (South of the River NIERS); Lieut. Jackson commanding the troop supporting the 1st Gordons, was killed by an enemy bazooka in the fierce house-to-house fighting (February 19th). Several days were now spent in mopping up the area, mainly in dealing with pillboxes; the infantry advancing South and South West until on February 28th the Division and the Regiment began a rest period. 'B' Squadron was still located with 153 Brigade at GRAFENTHAL when the Prime Minister visited the Highland Division, and at that Brigade Headquarters witnessed a parade of the pipes and drums of the Division.

A few days later the Regiment moved back into HOLLAND to DEURNE, near HELMOND, for a fortnight's rest.

34 Tank Brigade was placed in Second Army reserve for the Rhine crossing on March 24th, but it was never necessary to use it. 'B'Squadron left the Regiment on March 29th and joined 2nd Army Headquarters as a guard squadron in GERMANY. It went right up to the ELBE and part of the Squadron crossed that river carrying out its protective duties, it did not rejoin the Regiment until May 15th after the end of hostilities.

The Regiment, less 'B' Squadron, did not cross the RHINE until April 7th, when it took over the internal security of an area south of BOCHOLT. Later, a second area, NORTH of MUNSTER, was taken over and Headquarters established at NORDWALDE. On May 31st the Regiment moved and concentrated in a large Barracks just West of MUNSTER.

SECTION V — CONCLUSION

I had hoped to be able to write a Part II to this little history recording the Regiment's service in the closing stages of the JAPANESE WAR. But that was not to be as I shall briefly relate below.

While concentrated at MUNSTER, we learnt our orders in June 45. We were to go to SEAC as a Tank Battalion (Light) together with other units of our old Bde, the 34th Armoured Bde. To prepare us for the new theatre much reorganization was necessary, and we lost some 300 officers and men of early release groups, taking in their place an equivalent number by rank and trade from the 147 Regiment R. A. C., a converted Battalion of the Hampshire Regiment. 'B' Squadron became the "Hampshire Squadron" under Major J. A. H. Box, and the remainder of the Hampshire intake was distributed throughout the rest of the Regiment.

Lt. Col. H. H. K. Rowe, now awarded the D. S. O., left us at this time to take Command of the Rhine Army R. A. C. Training Regiment. Lt.-Col. R. H. Taite, who had been one of the original Company Commanders in the Regiment when it was the 50th Holding Battalion King's Own in 1940, and again Company Commander and Regimental Second-in-Command of the 10th Battalion and Second-in-Command of the Regiment when renamed 151 Regiment R. A. C. on conversion in 1942, was posted and assumed Command. Many of the old King's Own Officers and ORs accompanied Lt. Col. Rowe to his new Command, and have found there a happy home for the last few months of their Army service.

For a short while training in normal tank warfare went on apace with special training based on lessons already learnt in the Far Eastern Theatre, together with the usual training in precautions against tropical diseases and malaria. Never had a Regiment possessed such magnificent material, with practically every man trade-tested and mustered in one or more trades and battle experienced to boot. The average age, including the CO, QM, WO's, and Senior Ranks was about 24 years.

But our enthusiasm for battle was short lived. The Atom Bomb caused the sudden collapse of JAPAN and diverted our thoughts and energies towards peace and civil life. A few weeks of uncertainty ended in the new decision that we would not sail for SEAC but would remain in BAOR as a "de-horsed" Armoured Regiment or occupational "equivalent battalion". Our tanks were removed from us and we became in effect "black-hatted infantry".

I will not bore you with any long description of our life as an occupational unit, or of our duties thus taken on. Sufficient to say that all commitments given to us were faithfully performed but that most of our energies were turned towards sport and physical fitness, welfare and entertainments, preparation and education for civil life. During August we had to decentralize with HQ and 'A' Squadrons in MUNSTER, 'B' Squadron out at EVERSWINKEL and 'C' Squadron out at BILLERBECK. At the end of September we moved again and established ourselves with HQ at LAGGENBECK near OSNABRUCK and 'A', 'B' and 'C' Squadrons at LENGERICH.

In October 1945 another reorganization, on the reverse principle, was carried out. Again some 300 officers and men, this time of late release groups, left us to keep going the regular units of the 7th Armoured Division. In replacement we received NCO's and men of the earlier release groups from those same units, namely 5th Royal Inniskilling Dragoon Guards, 8th King's Royal Irish Hussars, 1st Royal Tank Regiment and 5th Royal Tank Regiment. Later also we received other small drafts from the 4/7th Dragoon Guards, 1st Fife and Forfar Yeomanry, 4th Royal Tank Regiment, 9th Royal Tank Regiment, 11th Royal Tank Regiment, and the 49th Armoured Personnel Carrier Regiment. Very few men now remain of those originally enlisted with the King's Own prior to conversion to R. A. C. in 1942.

In October also the "King's Own College" opened in LENGERICH under the guidance of Major B. H. Wilson MBE and Capt. C. H. Deakin MC. Some 20 different subjects were offered to the men and some 500 men availed themselves of the offer. Excellent results were obtained.

Early in 1946 the reorganization of the Army of Occupation, due to the release programme and the final settlement of what forces are to remain in Germany, caused a considerable move round among units of the Brigade. We have been lucky in that this has only meant the move of 'C' Squadron from LENGERICH to WESTERKAPPELN. But we ourselves are now in the throes of preparing for "suspended animation", and by the end of February 1946 the 107 Regiment R. A. C. (King's Own) will have passed into the pages of history.

As an Epitaph I would like to conclude with these remarks. Thanks to a good start made under Lt.-Col. Crow's command, this Regiment — or Battalion — call it what you will has been well known throughout for its smartness of discipline and turnout, its military efficiency, and the friendly spirit of comradeship to be found throughout all ranks. Despite its present diluted state of officers and men and despite intakes of be-medalled veterans of many other Regiments, it has retained to the end very noticeably its indentity as a unit, and, though doubtless with a few pangs of regret here and there, disperses to civil life and other units "clean, sober and properly dressed".

ROLL OF OFFICERS AND OTHERS RANKS KILLED IN ACTION

Officers:

Date	Number	Rank	Name	Sqn.
15/ 7/44	186 962	Lieut	Turner T.	B
21/ 7/44	92 300	Lieut	Snook F. J. MBE	B
8/ 8/44	268 029	Lieut	Hopkins N. J.	A
8/ 8/44	284 458	Lieut	Snell J. D. B.	A
8/ 8/44	156 136	Capt	Parker T. G.	C
14/ 8/44	292 171	Lieut	Fothergill J. A.	B
27/10/44	113 720	Capt	MacKenna R. A.	B
28/10/44	285 438	Lieut	Sanders E. A.	Bde L. O.
3/12/44	237 969	Capt	Julius A. C. S.	B
13/ 2/45	315 901	Lieut	Walker J. H.	B
19/ 2/45	262 369	Lieut	Jackson T. J.	B

Other Ranks:

Date	Number	Rank	Name	Sqn.
15/ 7/44	3 716 911	L/L/C	Turner H	B
15/ 7/44	3 969 186	Tpr	Stanbridge R.	B
16/ 7/44	14 220 782	Tpr	Connor J.	HQ
17/ 7/44	7 953 234	Tpr	Davidson M.	B
17/ 7/44	14 383 396	Pte	Johnson J. (ACC)	B
17/ 7/44	3 716 909	Pte	Taylor W. (ACC)	B
17/ 7/44	2 380 585	Dvr	Kennedy J. B. (R. Sigs)	HQ
17/ 7/44	6 352 767	Tpr	Read T. J.	HQ
17/ 7/44	7 953 228	L/L/C	Barrass W.	A
18/ 7/44	3 716 889	Tpr	Barnes F	B

Date	Number	Rank	Name	Sqn.
8/ 8/44	3 714 500	L/C	Whitaker J.	C
8/ 8/44	3 716 801	Sgt	Davies C.	C
8/ 8/44	3 715 301	L/C	Kelly M.	C
8/ 8/44	7 940 230	Tpr	McLaughlan J.	C
8/ 8/44	5 193 959	Tpr	Clarke R. W.	A
8/ 8/44	7 957 924	Tpr	Wilson J.	A
8/ 8/44	7 951 428	Tpr	Ashford P.	A
8/ 8/44	14 573 208	Tpr	Humphreys J. D.	A
9/ 8/44	14 252 338	Tpr	Elliott N. R.	B
9/ 8/44	3 713 964	Sgt	Hill R. C.	B
9/ 8/44	3 714 137	Cpl	Eastwood W. E.	A
14/ 8/44	14 303 917	Tpr	Tidswell K.	B
14/ 8/44	14 227 439	Tpr	Shepherd J	B
14/ 8/44	3 716 975	Tpr	Sharratt G	B
9/10/44	3 708 759	L/C	Lowles A. D.	B
21/10/44	814 079	Cpl	Stackhouse T.	HQ
21/10/44	14 262 814	Tpr	Pile T.	HQ
21/10/44	14 270 022	Tpr	Robins A. W.	HQ
21/10/44	3 717 027	Tpr	Summerfield T.	A
22/10/44	3 010 406	RSM	Greig A.	HQ
22/10/44	6 028 176	Cpl	Craske H.	C
22/10/44	7 951 407	Tpr	McIntyre A. A.	C
26/10/44	14 262 288	Tpr	Midlane B.	C
11/11/44	3 715 748	Tpr	Birch J.	A
10/ 2/45	6 030 226	Tpr	Hales W. H. A.	C

WOUNDED IN ACTION AND SINCE DIED

Date	Number	Rank	Name	Sqn.
17/ 7/44	14 259 424	Tpr	Smith A. T.	A
17/ 7/44	3 716 956	L/C	Greenhalgh J.	B
7/ 8/44	3 714 449	Sgt	Atkinson T. N.	A
7/ 8/44	4 124 012	Tpr	Clowes J.	HQ
8/ 8/44	10 691 019	Dvr	Atherton J. (R. Sigs)	HQ
9/ 8/44	3 714 828	L/L/C	Morey J. W.	B
9/ 8/44	3 716 223	Cpl	Levene S.	B
21/10/44	6 032 117	Tpr	Frisby F. J.	HQ

MISSING — BELIEVED KILLED

Date	Number	Rank	Name	Sqn.
8/ 8/44	7 935 451	Cpl	Martin G.	C
9/ 8/44	7 953 342	Tpr	Hoyle A. J.	B
9/ 8/44	3 713 356	Tpr	Bamber J. E. C.	B
9/ 8/44	3 716 841	Tpr	Moran B.	C
9/ 8/44	3 716 668	Tpr	Taylor W.	C
11/11/44	3 713 796	Tpr	Anderton J.	A
11/11/44	3 716 959	Tpr	Jackson E.	A
11/11/44	3 716 292	L/C	Norris W.	A
11/11/44	4 914 166	Tpr	Latham F.	A

MISSING — BELIEVED PRISONERS OF WAR

Date	Number	Rank	Name	Sqn.
8/ 8/44	7 664 836	L/C	Judd E.	A

MISSING — NO DETAILS KNOWN

Date	Number	Rank	Name	Sqn.
16/ 7/44	3 714 023	L/C	Porter E.	HQ
8/ 8/44	3 715 734	Cpl	Farrar W.	A
8/ 8/44	7 957 910	Tpr	Phillips J.	A

PISONERS OF WAR

Date	Number	Rank	Name	Sqn.
8/ 8/44	14 367 859	Tpr	Auth C. E.	A
21/10/44	14 242 978	Tpr	Uttridge V. R.	HQ

REPORT ON RAID ON ESQUAY, 2ND AUGUST 1944

Reference Maps: — FRANCE 36/16 SE.
37/14 NE.

1. OBJECT

To identify enemy on Divisional front and, in particular to ascertain whether 10 Panzer Division had been withdrawn.

2. TROOPS

107 R. A. C.
'B' Company 4 WELCH Regiment.
Two troops 'C' Squadron 141 R. A. C. (Crocodiles)

3. PRELIMINARY

An 'O' Group was called at Headquarters, 160 Infantry Brigade at 1400 hrs, 2nd August, to consider method of realising above object.

At 1600 hrs it was decided to raid the BON REPOS Cross Roads and Northern edge of ESQUAY, and H hour was determined as 2100 hrs, 2nd August.

The simplicity of the plan enabled the attack to be mounted in the time available; but H hour could not have been earlier.

4. OUTLINE PLAN

a) To attack one company up ('B' Company), roughly astride the axis TOURMAUVILLE — BON REPOS Cross roads. This advance by company two platoons up. Start Line and Forming Up Point — road BARON—GAVRUS. First objective road running North East—South West through BON REPOS cross roads thence a maximum of 400 yards South East to ESQUAY if sufficent prisoners of war were not taken on the first objective.

(b) 'B' Squadron (Major Davies) 107 R. A. C., to give close support to advance of 'B' Company with two troops on the flanks of leading platoons; two more troops to move behind and echeloned inwards towards Centre Line. Headquarters behind with reserve troops. One troop of crocodiles to move behind leading troops in position of immediate availability.

(c) Artillery (Wind East North East. 10 miles per hour)
 (I) Smoke feature 112 on left flank of advance.
  Smoke feature FE DE MONDVILLE ahead of advance and down to valley of River GUIGNE.

(II) Smoke feature 120 ring contour ('SAUSAGE') from North of Evrecy to North East tip of feature. All smoke from H Hour to H plus 60.

(III) S t o n k s. Right main road immediately South West of Cross Roads BON REPOS to cover area triangle wood and embankment. Immediately North West of BON REPOS Cross roads covering BON REPOS buildings and road for 300 metres North East. Both Stonks H plus 18 to H plus 30.

(IV) C o n c e n t r a t i o n s. Lifting from stonks at H plus 30 to (right area) immediately West 500 metres of B in BAS D' ESQUAY and (on left) to "enemy digs and weapon pits" 953 613. Both concentrations H plus 30 to H plus 60.

(d) T a n k S u p p o r t. 'A' Squadron 107 R. A. C. to support from area North of Point 112 South West along road BON REPOS—EVRECY; giving full machine gun support from H to H plus 23. (36 Besas were put on to this task; each tank averaging from 6 to 7 belts of Besa each) 'C' Squadron 107 R. A. C. in counterattack reserve in area South of Wood GOURNEY on map.

5. THE ACTION

Forming up of 'B' Squadron and 'B' Company was only just completed in time, but there was not time to "marry up" Crocodiles with infantry.

OC 4 WELCH Regiment commanded from Rear 'B' Squadron HQ. OC 107 R. A. C. commanded from 'A' Squadron area North of Point 112.

The advance went off precisely on time, smoke being laid simultaneously on pre-arranged areas.

'A' Squadron left flank machine gun support sounded terrific and must certainly have kept many heads down.

On 'B' Squadron front there was a slight delay while infantry waited for the barrage, but when it came tank commanders say they consider our infantry must have suffered some casualties from it. Infantry get valuable cover at times from derelict tanks but may be criticized for using battle tanks on occasions — this is a very dangerous practice.

The advance was smooth and fairly uneventful until H plus 26 when the Crocodiles on the right were ordered on to their objective — the apex and Northern edge of Wood 942 613 and the house in the West corner of cross roads. The barrage was then just South of the road. Crocodiles completed task quickly and thoroughly but infantry were slow in getting on behind flame. Infantry platoon commander later admitted to tank squadron commander that at this stage he was temporarily "lost". Infantry however, went in about five minutes after first squirt. Smoke at this stage was good and tanks gave intimate support with 200 to 300 yards visibility.

Crocodiles on left went in at H plus 30 and were then about 100 yards from target — houses North East of cross roads. They passed the left leading troop and went in quickly, carrying out their task thoroughly. Infantry here were excellent and were in immediately behind the Crocodiles. Tank Commanders of left leading troops state infantry were under fairly heavy light machine gun fire here but did not attempt to indicate targets. Tanks stood off and engaged all hedges to their front with machine gun and high explosive.

One crocodile on left soon after burning BON REPOS houses was seen to catch alight in its belly pipe and when last seen was enveloped in flame. Leading troop on left insist that this was an eventual write-off.

Prisoners of War were then seen coming back by the forward tanks, who state that majority came from South of road; it is reported that some of the enemy were wearing British type steel helmets. At this stage, just before the infantry withdrawal, the leading and supporting tank troops engaged all buildings with Armoured Piercing and High Explosive.

The leading tank of the left forward troop reports that he was shot at by Armoured Piercing from area BON REPOS buildings. He vaguely discerned a tank there and thought it might be a captured Churchill. He stated there was definitely no tank there previously. On being interrogated the troop Corporal confirmed the incident and presence of a Churchill. All three tanks of this troop were hit by armoured piercing which was very probably APCBC 75 mm. The Corporal got off three to four rounds at it before it was lost in smoke. The troop were highly indignant when it was suggested that they had had a private battle — they all reckoned this unknown tank got off about twelve rounds. The gunner of the troop Corporal's tank claims a certain hit.

Infantry withdrew at H plus 50 and the leading tank troops were ordered to withdraw through support troops at H plus 60.

Commander 'B' Company was wounded about H plus 40 and was evacuated by the centre line in a carrier.

Commander 'B' Squadron tried to get in touch with infantry over command net, but as everything was under control and withdrawal imminent he did not persevere.

Squadron commander and leading troops were convinced that there was an enemy anti-tank gun in area cross roads but no confirmation was forthcoming. It was, however, confirmed that this was not the Churchill tank.

Withdrawal of tanks went according to plan but CHEUX start line could not be seen until just South of original Start Line. Unfortunately one Crocodile lost a track on our uncharted minefield at 935 624 and a Churchill suffered similarly later Both are now recovered. It is thought that the Crocodile lost by the BON REPOS cross roads was mined before it brewed up, but this is not confirmed.

Finally there was no confirmation of any dug in tank or pit just NORTH of the Orchard at 942 613; a rumour prevalent prior to the advance.

6. REMARKS

As far as tanks are concerned, smoke was of great value. They had to thicken up patches periodically here and there but generally speaking were able to operate effectively at short range. Long range 88's were given no chance of engaging our tanks.

The simplicity of the plan was the main reason for the attack going in to time and the success of the operation.

The Regimental Intelligence Officer (Lieut. Edwards) was severely wounded and his scout car knocked out, when directing the machine gun fire 'A' Squadron from the left flank.

7. CASULTIES
   (a) *107 R. A. C.*
        Tanks — Nil.
        Personnel: Killed — Nil. Wounded — One Officer.
   (b) 'C' Squadron 141 R. A. C.
        Tanks — — One brewed up.
        Personel: Nil.

REPORTS FROM 'B' SQUADRON ON MINOR ACTIONS From 16—18 AUG 1944

Attack on ST. MARC D'OUILLY on 16th August 1944

In the evening of the 15th August 1944, it was decided to occupy the village of St. MARC D'OUILLY at first light 16th August 1944. Prisoner of war reports stated that the enemy had withdrawn, but patrols of the ROYALS and NORTH STAFFORDSHIRES reported the village held by a Company approximately.

Based on this information it was decided to put in a Company attack supported by the tanks. In this operation three troops were employed. No 6 troop was brought up to the outskirts of the village under cover of the incoming mist, and Nos 9 and 10 Troops were positioned on high ground North of the village. The village was then bombarded for about twenty minutes. All houses known to be occupied were engaged and all dug in positions on the high ground also engaged. The shoot was mostly direct and very successful. The target area was then engaged by Besa which started numerous fires. The tanks then put down. smoke and the infantry and armoured cars entered the village.

The enemy had withdrawn from the village, but still held the high ground.

There was considerable shelling and mortaring, which forced the infantry and armoured cars to withdraw. The Battalion Commander then decided that he would have to mount a Battalion attack the following day.

Enemy was heard mortaring to the South West.

The operation from a tank point of view was a success despite that fact that the infantry could not remain in the village.

There were no tank casualties.

Attack in area of LES ISLES BARDEL with 7th NORFOLKS on 17 AUGUST

At 0800 hrs, 17th August 1944, 'B' Sqadron 107 R.A.C. was placed under command of 177th Infantry Brigade. At a Brigade 'O' Group at 0900 hrs the Squadron was placed in support of

7th NORFOLKS, and were at half an hours notice to move.

At about mid-day we were ordered to attend an 'O' Group with 7th Norfolks at road junction 024309.

The Norfolks, who had been advancing South from Le MESNIL VILLEMENT had been held up by strong opposition from high ground at 033285.

The Battalion Commander had decided to put in an attack with a Company supported by a Squadron of tanks.

The attack was carefully tied up and a sound artillery plan laid on. There was time for a detailed reconnaissance and Platoon commanders and Troop leaders saw the ground together.

Forming Up Point	— 024 306
Start Line	— Track South of Forming up Point.
Objective	— High ground 033295.
H Hour	— 1800 hours.
Formation	— 10 Troop 9 Troop
	HQ
	6 Troop 8 Troop

Everything went according to plan, tanks and infantry crossed the Start Line on time. The infantry were held up by machine gun posts which the tanks soon dealt with. About 20 prisoners were taken and many Huns were killed. 95 did a smoke task on left flank and an H. E. shoot MENIL HERMEL.

The infantry gained their objective in about 30 minutes.

S. P. 17 pounders, in support of the squadron moved up on to objective and all but two troops of tanks were released to Rear Rally.

Infantry 17 pounders and 6 pounders were up fairly quickly and tanks were released to Rear Rally before dark.

There were no tank casualties.

Advance trough MENIL HERMEL on 18 August 1944.

Composite 'B' Squadron 107 R. A. C. arranged to support NORFOLKS to wood North West of MENIL HERMEL. Before tanks were up in position the Commanding Officer of the NORFOLKS decided to put in the attack as there appeared to be no opposition.

The wood was clear of enemy and 'B' Squadron came under command of 5th South Staffordshire Regiment and tied up for an advance from the wood through MENIL HERMEL to point 207 (MR. 068274).

The Squadron consisted of 3 Troop, 1 Troop, Squadron Headquarters, and in support a Troop of Self Propelled Guns.

MENIL HERMEL was taken without opposition. The road was mined on the far side of the village and tanks were forced to deploy on to the left of the road. More mines in belts were encountered in the fields and only a short advance was made. Three tanks struck mines, and two on the mines were subsequently hit by small bazookas after the crew had evacuated. One tank brewed up. It was impossible to support the infantry further forward and they dug in a short distance from the objective. The tanks were released at last light and withdrew to harbour near Forming Up Point.

Casualties — Three tanks on mines.

One Officer wounded by shrapnel while clearing minebelt. Two Other Ranks wounded, one by mine blast when inside tank and one by shrapnel.

The ATTACK ON LE HAVRE

In the initial planning for the attack on LE HAVRE 107 Regiment, was placed in support of 147 Infantry Brigade in 49 Division.

107 R. A. C. was given the task of supporting one Battalion of this Brigade (7th Duke of Wellington's Regiment) in an attack to capture the high ground 536283 to 544280.

The Regiment concentrated in area 593 327 on the night 10th/11th September 1944.

On the morning 11th September, progress of remaining Battalions of 147 Infantry Brigade was held up by extensive minefields on all roads and tracks running from MONTEVILLERS to area 542305.

The infantry were not prepared to push forward to carry out their original tasks until such time as these roads and tracks had been cleared, accordingly the attack with the Duke of Wellington's did not go in as anticipated on the morning of 11th September..

At approximately 1700 hrs, 'A' Squadron were ordered to take 3 troops across the river on to the high ground in area 536 288 to give help in mopping up to the Royal Scots Fusiliers. This was done, although the Infantry Brigade Commander had said that the Scots Fusiliers were getting forward allright and did not require tank support. On arrival of O. C. 'A' Squadron and these three troops in that area it as found that the Scots Fusiliers were in dire need of tank support and accordingly the one troop which had proceeded with Commander 34 Tank Brigade into the outskirts of LE HAVRE was recalled, and together with the remaining Troop of 'A' Squadron, was sent over the river to join 'A' Squadron.

This Squadron had a good shoot against enemy machine gun positions in the area 538284 and 543281 killing and capturing quite a number of Huns and driving many more over the edge of the escarpment down to 9th Royal Tank Regiment area where it was understood they surrendered.

At 1845 hrs 'C' Squadron with under command six Crocodiles, was ordered to support an attack of the 7 th Duke of Wellington's Regiment to clear the buildings in the area 530284. This attack was got under way but had not procceded far before owing to failing light it had to be stopped.

The tanks rallied back to area 531 298 where they remained with 'A' Squadron for the night. The 7th Duke of Wellington's continuing to move through the badly bombed built up area during that night to obtain their objective which was the area 530 284.

On the morning 12th September, some enemy had returned to the area 539 283 and considerable Spandau and light Ack Ack fire was coming from that direction. One 20 mm site actually having the nerve to fire at an Air Observation Plane and a Dakota which passed over in that area. Accordingly 'C' Squadron were moved to that area and completed, with the company of 7 Duke of Wellington's the mopping up of that area. This was done sastifactorily, the light automatic in question being put out of action by 75 mm fire. 'C' Squadron was then ordered to take up hull down positions to support by fire, from the high ground, the mopping up of the area South of the canal VAUBAN.

Their particular task was enemy mortar sites in the area 540 255. A few mortar posts were engaged but definite results could not be obtained owing to the distance.

At approximately 1300 hrs the Regiment was released by 147 Infantry Brigade, the operation having been concluded, and the Regiment reverted to 34 Tank Brigade and rear-rallied.

REPORT ON RAID in ST OEDENRODE AREA (FROM 'C' SQUADRON)

Raid on the Red House

On the evening of 8th October 1944, the Squadron was informed that it was allotted to 1/5th WELSH REGIMENT to partake in a raid on a troublesome German Platoon position in two houses at 423 362.

The Squadron Commander met the Commanding Officer of the infantry battalion the next morning and owing to heavy mist was able to carry out extensive reconnaissance unseen.

H hour was fixed for 1500 hrs, at which time the tanks which were to move up slowly on minor tracks, to conceal noise, were to debouch on to the road ST OEDENROADE—SCHINDEL and move as fast as possible to the forward company position at Cross roads 418 358.

No. 3 Troop were to debouch first and move to the left of these buildings, followed by 4 Troop to the right. No frontal movement could be carried out owing to a ditch forming an obstacle across the front some 200 yards in front of the houses.

As soon as the houses had been shot up by the tanks two WASPS were to attack the slit trenches around the houses with flame, and 18 Platoon, 'D' Company were to assault from the front. The whole operation was to be covered with a smoke screen across the rear of the houses to protect the tanks and two field and one medium regiment were in support. Squadron HQ and 5 Troop were in reserve in the area forward of the MONASTERY 425 346.

The whole plan and timings worked perfectly, except that the flame of the right hand flamethrower did not ignite, but the left had played on to it and set it on fire. The whole operation was completed by 1545 hrs, and no casualties of any kind were sustained by our forces. Enemy reaction was limited to about twelve reounds of shell fire. One prisoner of war was captured, and a number of enemy dead seen, the total not being ascertainable.

Prisoner of war stated that the area was a Company position, which had suffered heavy casualties from mortar and shell fire. Approximately six Germans were seen to escape; it is thought the remainder were made casualties.

REPORTS ON ACTIONS WITH CLARKEFORCE FROM 20th—29th OCTOBER 1944

20th October

At 0600 hrs the Regiment moved to concentration area at ST LEONARD and on the capture of STAPELJELLE area by 56 Infantry Brigade supported by 9 R. T. R. the Regiment was passed through with the object of capturing WUESTWEZEL. The Regiment had under command one Company of Infantry, one Troop of Crocodiles, and one Troop of Self-Propelled Anti tank guns.

The Regiment moved one up, the order of march being 'B', 'A', 'C' Squadron ferrying the infantry.

The Regiment centre line was road junction 850 139, road junction 841 158, road junction 827 167 WUESTWEZEL.

The Regiment was launched at approximately 1600 hrs and reached road junction 841 158 at approx 1700 hrs where 'B' Squadron was ordered to take up a position North East to cover this road junction with half squadron whilst the remaining half squadron pushed on quickly to secure the crossing at STONE BRIDGE. Meanwhile the Reconnaissance Troop, which had had difficulty in coming up the centre line owing to the bad tank going, was also pushed forward to cross the bridge. Enemy transport travelling on the main road North East from STONE BRIDGE was engaged, at least one wheeled vehicle was set alight and a small number of prisoners taken. Having crossed STONE BRIDGE 'B' Squadron was ordered to take up a position facing NORTH and NORTH WEST forming a bridgehead while 'A' was passed through to take up a defensive position SOUTH and WEST of the bridge to allow the passage of 'C' Squadron and its infantry down the main road to clear WUSTWEZEL. By the time 'B' and 'A' Squadrons were over STONE BRIDGE it was dark, however, the Regiment pushed on and the infantry supported by tanks commenced clearing WUESTWEZEL in the dark. Quite a number of prisoners were taken. Meanwhile a patrol was sent South East along the WUESTWEZEL—BRECHT road to ascertain the condition of the bridge at 827 122, but was unable to get as far as that owing to finding the road flooded.

At 2100 hrs the Regiment was in defensive positions and occupying WUESTWEZEL. At 2200 hrs it was ordered to move out and take up a position in the area 793 153 to block roads in that area. This was done, the Regiment meeting minor opposition during the move, such as sniping and in one case bazooka fire. The night was pitch dark, it was raining and there was no moon, accordingly movement at that time along the WUSTWEZEL—NIEUWMOER 7619 road was very slow. The Reconnaissance Troop, which had gone ahead to reconnoitre a suitable area for harbouring, met a road block of trees across the road and reported a number of Huns in the neighbouring houses, a number of which were taken prisoner. The road block was cleared by the leading Churchills. At 0300 hrs the Regiment settled down into harbour

Sqn.	Enemy Vehicles/ Weapons knocked out		Enemy Vehicles/ Weapons suspected knocked out	
	SPs	others	SPs	others
B		2 A/Tk guns		
C		1 machine gun		
Recce Tp		2 Staff cars (1 captured)		
TOTALS				

Sqn.	Prisoners of War	Own Casualties			
		Offrs Killed	Offrs Wounded	Other Ranks Killed	Other Ranks Wounded
B	4				2
C	9				
Recce Tp	4 Offrs 11 ORs				
TOTALS	4 Offrs 24 ORs				2

21st October

The Regiment 'stood to' at 0545 hrs and at approximately 0800 hrs was ordered to assume the advance to NIEUWMOER. Order of March 'A', 'B', 'C' the latter Squadron still ferrying the infantry. There was no reconnaissance in front of the leading Squadron by the Reconnaissance Troop owing to the fact that that they had run out of petrol as no supplies could be brought up the previous night. 'A' Squadron of 49th Division preceded the leading Squadron of tanks and found the Bridge at 765 185 blown and accordingly sent troops out to either flank to find a way around. These troops were each backed up by a troop of tanks. Whilst reconnoitring the main bridge the Squadron Leader's Tank was fired on by 75 mm SP guns from NIEUWMOER village, receiving six hits without penetration at the same time other SP guns engaged the Reconnaissance Troops and tank troops on the flanks brewing up two carriers on the left.

'A' Squadron was ordered to proceed round the left flank and cut off the Village of NIEUWMOER from the NORTH. The movement to the left from the main road off the Regiment Centre line was in full view of the enemy SPs and entailed the use of smoke. When leading elements of 'A' Squadron came into the west edge of the village, the advance was slowed up by fire from two SPs which were in well concealed positions. One Churchill tank brewed up, one Officer Tank Commander and One Other Rank being wounded and one Other Rank killed. This slow progress was chiefly due to the inexperience in the method of dealing with enemy SPs by use of smoke to close with the enemy. By 1600 hrs 'A' Squadron were to the West of the village and 'C' Squadron and supporting infantry were launched to clear the village. The enemy brought down defensive fire on the village whilst it was being cleared causing a few infantry casualties. 'A' Squadron had been ordered to push round to the North of the village to cut the main road North. As soon as the clearance of the village was well in hand the Reconnaissance Troop was ordered to follow 'A' Squadron and observe from static positions the forward edges of the wood at 753 209. Unfortunately owing to the fact that 'A' Squadron was slow in moving to the north and the Reconnaissance Troop Leader not paying sufficient detail to map reading believing that he would find 'A' Squadron to the North of the Village, the Reconnaisance Troop proceded to the North of the Village quickly and the Troop Leader's tank passed right into the wood before he realised his mistake. The wood contained enemy infantry and at least three enemy SPs which proceeded to knock out four light tanks, three of which brewed up. The Reconnaissance Troop lost 3 Other Ranks killed inside one light tank, one missing from the Troop Leader's tank, and two others in the Troop Leader's tank were badly wounded. The Troop Leader escaped by running back down a ditch, first of all having seen that his crew were safely out of their burning vehicle. RHQ Troop which was following the Reconnaissance Troop closely was engaged by SPs from this wood and withdrew under cover of smoke. The Regiment rallied in the village of NIEUWMOER for the night of 21st October.

Sqn.	Enemy Vehicles/ Weapons knocked out		Enemy Vehicles/ Weapons suspected knocked out		Prisoners of War
	SPs	others	SPs	others	
A	1		1	1 A/Tk gun	30
B					
C					3
Recce		1 car &			
Tp		1 Amb captured			10
TOTALS	1		1		43

Sqn.	Own Casualties				Own Tanks knocked out
	Offrs Killed	Offrs Wounded	Other Ranks Killed	Other Ranks Wounded	
A		1	1	5	3
B				1	1
C				1	
Recce					
Tp			3	2	4
			(1 missing)		
TOTALS		1	4	9	8
			+ (1 missing)		

22nd October

On 22nd October the Regiment was ordered to cut the road NIEUWMOER—ESSCHEN to the North of SCHRIEK 745 218. This was done by an advance through VISSCHENHEUVEL—BREEDESTRAAT where the enemy infantry and SPs were successfully engaged. The leading Squadron 'C' Squadron, lost one tank, brewed up.

Having cut the road to the North of the wood at 7521 the canal on the South East edge of the wood was bridged by a Bridge layer and the Regiment was ordered to harbour that night in the area North West of the Wood. One troop of 'A' Squadron was detailed to assist in the defence of the road running EAST through NIEUWMOER where it remained engaging 2 enemy SPs one of which it knocked out.

During this day a portion of the Regiment's 'A' Echelon was ambushed near 760 172 — casualties to personnel being RSM Greig killed, 2 wounded and 11 prisoners. The 2 wounded and 11 prisoners being released next day after an attack on this position.

Sqn.	Enemy Vehicles/ Weapons knocked out		Enemy Vehicles/ Weapons suspected knocked out		Prisoners of War
	SPs	others	SPs	others	
HQ.					
A	1				
B					
C	1				
	1 (by med gun fire)				
TOTALS	3				

Sqn.	Own Casualties				Own Tanks knocked out
	Offrs Killed	Offrs Wounded	Other Ranks Killed	Other Ranks Wounded	
HQ.			1	2	
A					
B		1			
C			2	1	1
TOTALS		1	3	3	1

41

23rd October

The Regiment took up defensive positions covering the main ESSCHEN—NIEUWMOER road in the area SCHRIEK until relieved by infantry. The infantry took over that evening and the Regiment rallied back to NIEUWMOER for the night arriving in the dark. An attack by Duke of Wellington Regiment supported by one Squadron 107 R. A. C. was ordered for the following morning.

Sqn.	Enemy Vehicles/ Weapons knocked out		Enemy Vehicles/ Weapons suspected knocked out		Prisoners of War
	SPs	others	SPs	others	
HQ					
A			1		
B					
C					
TOTALS			1		

Sqn.	Own Casualties				Own Tanks knocked out
	Offrs Killed	Offrs Wounded	Other Ranks Killed	Other Ranks Wounded	
HQ				1	
A		1			1
B				1	
C				2	
TOTALS		1		4	1

24th October

At first light reconnaissance was carried out for the attack to capture the area SCHANKER. At 1000 hrs the attack went in in 2 companies up supported by 'C' Squadron 107 R. A. C. The attack was succesful the infantry having few casualties.
At 1530 hrs the infantry anti-tank guns were in position being very late in coming up. 'C' Squadron was withdrawn to rear rally at NIEUWMOER for the night. At 1630 hrs orders were received to move the whole Regiment to the village of ACHTERBROEK for the night. This was done. Some enemy mediums shelled the village four times during the night but there were no casualties to men or vehicles.

Sqn.	Enemy Vehicles/ Weapons knocked out		Enemy Vehicles/ Weapons suspected knocked out		Prisoners of War
	SPs	others	SPs	others	
C					59

25th October

The day was spent in planning a further advance to seize the area BREMBOSCH 7026.

26th October

At 0600 hrs the Regiment moved out to a concentration area in he railway yard at ESSCHEN. At approx 10 000 hrs the Regiment was launched on its objective passing through elements of 56 Infantry Brigade who had previously captured NISPEN area in a night advance.
On reaching BREMBOSCH area accurate fire was met from enemy SPs. One SP was hit, three 'C' Squadron tanks were knocked out (one being the Squadron Leader's tank). A number of prisoners were captured and the Regiment harboured for the night in the area BREMBOSCH under accurate enemy defensive fire, medium and mortar fire from time to time. 'B' and 'C' Squadron Leader's tanks were hit by enemy SP. 'B' Squadron Leader severly wounded and 2 members of his crew wounded.

Sqn.	Enemy Vehicles/ Weapons knocked out		Enemy Vehicles/ knocked out Weapons suspected		Prisoners of War
	SPs	others	SPs	others	
A	1				
B					40
C	1	1 A/Tk gun			30
Attd SPs					
TOTALS	2	1			70

Sqn.	Own Casualties				Own Tanks knocked out
	Offrs Killed	Offrs Wounded	Other Ranks Killed	Other Ranks Wounded	
A					
B		2		1	1
C			1	1	3
Attd SPs					1·SP knocked out
TOTALS		2	1	2	4 tanks 1 SP

27th October

Regimental dispositions this day were as follows:

'A' Squadron — area 703 267 with company of Royal Scots Fusiliers on tanks.

'B' Squadron —
  a) 2 troops and Squadron HQ area houses 698 272 (later one of these troops moved forward to protect bulldozer on either side

b) Remainder of 'B' Squadron area KOPPENHOFF 701 277 — task — cover North and North East approaches.

'C' Squadron —
  a) 2 troops area houses 708 274 in support Reconnaissance Regiment — task — cover North-East and East approaches.
  b) Remainder 'C' Squadron area 703 267 — task — to cross bridge at 696 275 and form bridgehead.

At 0800 hrs an attack was put in by 2 companies of the Leicester Regiment supported by half 'B' Squadron 107 R. A. C. to cross anti tank ditch and road block on the road BREMBOSCH —WOUWSHE HIL. The infantry supported by fire from 'B' Squadron crossed the ditch by means of ladders under accurate enemy small arms fire and for med a small bridgehead. The remaining half of 'B' Squadron and half of 'C' Squadron found protection to the North to cover this operation which faced WEST. Two Troops of 'C' Squadron had been ordered to area 708 274 to support a Squadron of Reconnaissance which was reconnoitring the road BREMBOSCH—TOLBERG. A bulldozer was then brought down to the obstacle and attempted to clear it by pulling loose rubble on to the concrete obstacle. This proved unsatisfactory so the top of the obstacle was knocked off by AP and HE fire from tanks and SP guns. This work was carried out under accurate sniping from the enemy from positions in the surrounding fields and open country. Capt MacKenna, Reconnaissance Officer of 'B Squadron was killed by a ricochet whilst dismounted and reconnoitring the obstacle.

At 1100 hrs the first Tank was over the obstacle. The Regiment then passed over and having assisted the Infantry to clear the houses and surrounding fields at the WARBERG BRIDGE Area, the Regiment proceeded to WOUWSHE HIL where a plan was made to take OOSTLAAR that night.

Whilst in this Area the Regiment came under accurate enemy shell and mortar fire but no casualties to the Infantry with Tanks were sustained.

At approx 1400 hrs the Regiment moved off to OOSTLAAR via HAINK 6928. The Regiment moved across country and was engaged by enemy SPs on the way. One Tank being brewed up and one hit. Smoke was laid and the Regiment arrived at HAINK where a pause was made to issue orders for the final stages of the move across country to OOSTLAAR; this entailed the move across the front of the enemy SPs which were sighted in the area 694 292 and 697 289 and 702 287. Just prior to moving off the Regiment was engaged by enemy SPs at comparitively close range. One Tank was brewed up. At the same time the enemy brought strong concentration of medium gun fire on to the locality.

Smoke was laid and the enemy SPs engaged, one being knocked out. Delay in moving from HAINK was now caused by a number of tanks becoming either bogged in bad ground or minor engine trouble caused through continuous days fighting with little time for maintenance. After approx half and hour, during which time the Regiment was stonked by HE and shot at by AP alternatively, the order was given for the Regiment to move across country to OOSTLAAR under cover of smoke screens on either flank. This move was carried out in good order and no tanks were left behind. The regiment arrived as dark was falling at OOSTLAAR and took up pre-arranged positions round farm buildings in that area. The Regiment harboured for the night in that area whilst the Infantry Company, who had been ferried on 'A' Squadron Tanks, proceeded to clear the road to the NW of WOUW. An enemy SP was known to be at the road and railway crossing and also enemy infantry had been seen digging 600 yards to the West in AKKER

Sqn.	Enemy Vehicles/ Weapons knocked out		Enemy Vehicles/ Weapons suspected knocked out		Prisoners of War
	SPs	others	SPs	others	
A	1				
B					
Attd SPs					30
TOTALS	1				30

Sqn.	Own Casualties				Own Tanks knocked out
	Offrs Killed	Offrs Wounded	Other Ranks Killed	Other Ranks Wounded	
A					1
B	1				2
Attd SPs					1 SP
TOTALS	1				1 SP 3 Tanks

28th October

At 0645 hrs, as it got light, an enemy SP opened up on 'C' Squadron tanks and Transport which was replenishing tanks at that time, knocking out one tank and destroying three vehicles by fire. 'C' Squadron and RHQ were withdrawn behind 'A' Squadron under cover of smoke. One 17 pounder SP being destroyed by an enemy 88 mm SP during this withdrawal.

At 0815 hrs an attack on WOUW was put in by the Royal Scots Fusiliers supported by 107 R. A. C.

The first stage of the attack was a thrust NW to AKKER. This proceeded satisfactorily and the Infantry supported by Tanks out the road WOUW—BERGEN OP ZOOM at approx 1100 hrs. Enemy SPs were known to be in WOUW and EAST of the Advance, but well laid smoke enabled the leading troops of tanks to get on to the road without casualties. The enemy SPs kept up continual HE and AP fire whenever targets showed themselves. Our 2 remaining 17 pounder SPs engaged and knocked out one enemy SP in the area of the brickworks 685 293. Unfortunately in the process one of these 2 SPs was knocked out. A number of Prisoners were taken in WOUW and the infantry supported by 'A' Squadron completed the clearance of the village by 1600 hrs. The Regiment harboured in WOUW for the night.

Sqn.	Enemy Vehicles/ Weapons knocked out		Enemy Vehicles/ Weapons suspected knocked out		Prisoners of War
	SPs	others	SPs	others	
A					
B					
C					
Attd SPs	1				
TOTALS	1				

Sqn.	Own Casualties				Own Tanks knocked out
	Offrs Killed	Offrs Wounded	Other Ranks Killed	Other Ranks Wounded	
A					1
B				3	1
					2—½ Tracks
C				3	1—3 Tonner
Attd SPs					2 SPs
TOTALS				6	2 Tanks
					1—3 Tonner
					2—½ Tracks
					2 SPs

29th October

All available tanks except for those necessary for guarding WEST of WOUW were placed in position to support attack by 146 Brigade supported by 9 R Tks, to cut the road WOUW—ROOSENDAAL at BOEINK. 3 enemy SPs were observed and engaged. Hits were observed on one of them. Enemy transport proceeding EAST of ROOSENDAAL were also engaged by 95 mm and supporting artillery.

Sqn.	Enemy Vehicles/ Weapons knocked out		Enemy Vehicles/ Weapons suspected knocked out		Prisoners of War
	SPs	others	SPs	others	
A			1		
TOTALS			1		

Sqn.	Own Casualties				Own Tanks knocked out
	Offrs Killed	Offrs Wounded	Other Ranks Killed	Other Ranks Wounded	
B				1	
TOTALS				1	

GRAND TOTAL BY SQUADRONS

Sqn.	Enemy Vehicles/ Weapons knocked out		Enemy Vehicles/ Weopons suspected knocked out		Prisoners of War
	SPs	others	SPs	others	
HQ		2 Staff Cars (1 captured) 1 Car. 1 Amb (Car)			4 Offrs 21 ORs
A	4		3	1 A/Tk gun	30 ORs
B		2 A/TK guns			74 ORs
C	3	1 machine gun			101 ORs
Attd SPs	1	1 A/Tk gun			
TOTALS	8		3		230

Sqn.	Own Casualties				Own Tanks knocked out
	Offrs Killed	Offrs Wounded	Other Ranks Killed	Other Ranks Wounded	
HQ			4	5 (plus 1 missing)	4 (Stuarts)
A		2	1	5	6 Tanks
B	1	3		9	5 Tanks
C			3	8	2—½ Tracks 4 Tanks 1—3 Tonner
Attd SPs					4 SPs
TOTALS	1	5	8	27 (plus 1 missing)	19 Tanks 4 SPs 2—½ Tracks 1—3 Tonner

REPORT ON ACTION WITH 44 INFANTRY BRIGADE (15th SCOTTISH DIVISION) IN CAPTURE OF BLERICK

44 Infantry Brigade supported by 2 Squadrons 107 R.A.C., 1 Flail Regiment (22 DRAGOONS), 2 Squadrons A.V.R.E.'s and 1 Regiment KANGAROOS was ordered to capture BLERICK on 3rd December 1944.

Owing to the defensive belt of mines and the anti tank ditch, the attack was to take place in two phases as follows: —

(Phase I) The clearing of obstacles by the armour under command Brigadier Knight.

(Phase II) The capture of the town of BLERICK by 44 Infantry Brigade supported by armour.

H Hour was 0745 hrs 3rd December 1944.

In spite of heavy rain the night before, the decision to continue with the attack was made by Brigadier Knight at 0001 hrs 3rd December.

At 0525 hrs the supporting artillery counter battery concentration commenced, timed to cover the noise of the mass of armour moving forward to the Forming Up Points.

The attack was to be made on a two battalion front. The centre line of the left and Northernmost sector proved to be bad going as anticipated, and during the move forward of the armour 'B' Squadron 107 R.A.C. were invaluable in towing out bogged flails. It is quite certain that had it not been for this assistance by the Churchills no lanes could have been made on the left hand battalion front.

At H hour the armour moved over the Start Line to make —

(a) On each battalion Sector three lanes through a scattered minefield at the near side of the anti-tank ditch.

(b) Put an S.P. bridge down each lane over the anti tank ditch after which flails were to proceed over the ditch and flail further lane down through known mine belts on the enemy side of the ditch.

The whole of the operation was supported on each sector by a Squadron of 107 R.A.C., 'C' Squadron right, 'B' Squadron left.

On the right sector where there was better going, lanes and bridging was carried out satisfactorily. 'C' Squadron 107 R. A. C. losing their Reconnaissance Officer's tank on 2 mines when engaging some enemy in slit trenches. This was the only tank casualty of the Regiment during the operation.

On the left hand sector, the going not being so good there was delay in getting bridges over the obstacles, and in the case of one bridge it received two direct hits immediately on being laid and eventually only one bridge was maintained in this sector.

This completed the main armoured phase, and the infantry were called forward in KANGAROOS to pass through the lanes and over the bridges to attack BLERICK. The majority of the infantry were out over the bridges on the right hand sector. A very good smoke screen North of BLERICK and on both flanks of the attack was maintained by the supporting artillery, supplemented by tank smoke when necessary.

At no time was enemy AP fire encountered, but there was throughout the action continuous and accurate enemy artillery "stonking" on the nearside of the anti tank obstacle, where the supporting Churchills were in position.

At the very commencement of operations Capt. Buckenham commanding 'B' Squadron was severely wounded in the face by shell splinters and evacuated.

At approximately 1200 hrs permission was obtained from Brigadier Knight to thin out forward Churchill Squadrons.

At approximately 1345 hrs 'C' Squadron on the right sector were released and returned to Rear Rally at MAASBREE.

By this time two battalions of the Infantry Brigade were in position up to the River Maas on the right Sector and one battalion was half way into BLERICK on the left sector.

Two troops and Squadron HQ of 'B' Squadron /107 R. A. C. were detained in its supporting fire position in case assistance was required by the 4th Battalion of the Infantry Brigade, whose task was to come into line on the extreme left and clear the large factory North of BLERICK. Isolated pockets enemy of resistance were encountered by the infantry but they overcame these by themselves, since owing to the bad state of the ground the armour commander did not wish to pass Crocodiles and/or supporting Churchills over the bridges on the enemy side of the ditch unless it was absolutely necessary.

At 1530 hrs approximately, permission was obtained for 'B' Squadron to return to Rear Rally. On their return several tanks bogged on the very bad ground, but these were all hauled clear by the Regiment's Recovery vehicles, under the Regimental Technical Adjutant, before dark.

The Regiment moved to area NEDERWEERT on the night 3rd December, arriving approximately 1800 hrs. Unfortunately during the march back, Capt. A. C. S. Julius, 'B' Squadron's Reconnaissance Officer, was killed when his tank overturned beside the road when passing a stationary vehicle in the dark.

Total Casualties	Tanks	Personnel
	1 tank damaged by mines.	1 Officer wounded.
		1 Offier killed by accident
		2 Other Ranks wounded by shell splinters.

REPORT ON ACIONS WITH 51 HIGHLAND DIVISION FROM 8—28 FEB 45

PLAN

8th February

51 Highland Division attacked at 1030 hrs on a one Brigade front (154 Brigade) 2 Battalions up. Right 7th Black Watch, objective BREEDEWEG 766 524 and BRUUK 767 527. Left, 1st Black Watch, objective first Wood 778 527, second High Ground 788 524.

On capturing BREEDEWEG the 5/7th Gordons (153 Brigade under Command 154 Brigade) were to pass through 7th Black Watch and secure high ground 773 509. Thereafter 153 Brigade would pass through 7th Black Watch and 5/7th Gordons, turn west and clear up wooded area up to an including 752 508.

In the initial stages of the attack gaps were to be made on the right at 763 527 and 765 528, and on the left where there were two obstacles one gap was to be made over each obstacle at 776 533 and 779 531. 107 R. A. C. had under command for these gapping operations one Squadrons Flails, one Squadron A. V. R. E., S. and in reserve for mopping up, if required one Squadron Crocodiles (Fife and Forfar Yeomanry).

Allotment of Squadrons. 'B' Squadrons 107 R. A. C. to support 7th Black Watch and 5/7th Gordons in initial phase and 153 Brigade on passing through. 'A' Squadron 107 R. A. C. to support 152 Brigade in exploitation role in the REICHSWALD on D plus 1.

ATTACK

H hour was 1030 hrs on D Day, 8th February 1945, and the attack moved forward after a 5 hour artillery bombardment. From the outset it was realised that tanks would have difficulty in passing across country. Therefore a decision was made to pass armour, particulary Flail and A.V.R.E.'s, down road until past the anti-tank ditch and it was decided to make crossings on the roads.

On the right, Flails and A.V.R.E.'S carried out their drill perfectly and a bridge was laid at 763 526. On the centre crossing at 766 528 and 767 527 determined enemy opposition was met. one Flail tank being bazookoed and the road blocked. The infantry casualties were heavy, one Company Commander and one Platoon Commander being killed by snipers. The majority of 'B' Squadron were deflected through the right hand gap. Stiff opposition was met with at BREEDEWEG and GRAFWEGEN 762 522.

On the left 'A' Squadron supporting 1 Black Watch, made good headway until arriving at the first obstacle where an attempt was made to breach it at the track at 776 533. However, neither Flails nor the A.V.R.E. bridge layers could get down this track and tanks started to bog. Accordingly the tanks were deflected on the main road immediately North East, along which the Flails cleared the mines and the craters were bridged or facined by A.V.R.E. teams. Two troops of 'A' Squadrons were then passed over, but as difficulty was experienced in turning South East off the road to regain the centre line, the remainder of the Squadron were passed over the anti-tank ditch just North East of the road where a crossing had been made by teams of the flanking division. The going was exceedingly bad and two troops of 'A' Squadron became badly bogged. However, these were satisfactorily recovered that evening.

Meanwhile 'A' Squadron Leader and his Squadron, less these two troops, had contacted 1 Black Watch again and one troop was sent forward to assist the leading infantry to gain its second objective, the high ground at 788 524. This troop did very good work, killing a lot of Huns and 154 Brigade Commander stated that he did not wish any further tanks to be committed into the wood at this stage. Accordingly the remainder of 'A' Squadron harboured for the night at 783 527.

Meanwhile on the right flank a troop of 'B' Squadron overcame stiff enemy resistance which was holding up the infantry at 773 516, and pushed on with 5/7 Gordons to their objective, the high ground at 773 509.

A lot of mopping up had to be done now in the BREEDEWEG and GREFWEGEN area as determined enemy resistance was met in these locations, and by nightfall the 1st Gordons had reached area 759 508, but owing to the fact that small enemy pockets and Bazooka teams still existed in the fringes of the wood, 'B' Squadron were withdrawn after dark to the area 773 519 for maintenance and short rest. Mines had been met with by 'B' Squadron to the North West and West of the REICHSWALD and they had by this time suffered two tank casualties from mines.

CASUALTIES
8th February

Personnel	Killed	Wounded
Officers	—	Lt. Robertson 'B' (Sqn)
Other Ranks	—	6
Total	—	1 Offrs & 6 Other Ranks
Tanks	Mined 2	Penetrated Ap/Bazooka/Heavy HE —

Att Vehicles One Flail tank bazookoed and brewed up. One SP Anti-tank Gun mined.

9th February

At first light on 9th February one troop 'B' Squadron supported 5/7 Gordons to secure Cross Tracks 776 515, two troops 'B' Squadron continued to support 1st Gordons in their attacks to secure area 750 508 and to link up with the Canadians who had been holding high ground 745 515 prior to D-Day. In this they were successful, with the loss of one tank on a mine. In the afternoon 5 Black Watch pushed South down the causeway from 770 505 to the area 767 487, supported by long range 75 mm fire from 'B' Squadron's HQ and two troops on the high ground 766 505. 'B' Squadron harboured night 9/10 February in the area 765 508.

Also at first light elements of 152 Brigade had been brought up from their harbour area 737 528 and passed through BREEDEWEG and continued the assault into the REICHSWALD with as their objective approximately 788 512. One troop of C' Squadron supported the attack of this leading Battalion in their very difficult task in this close wooded country and in one small patch several hundred dead Hun were counted. No further troops of 'C' Squadron were allowed through that day by G. O. C. 51 Highland Division, owing to the bad state of the roads, one troop of 'B' Squadron was therefore placed under command O. C. 'C' Squadron.

Meanwhile on the left one troop of 'A' Squadron with the 7th Argyll & Sutherland Highlanders had pushed on to Cross tracks 795 518, this troop again accounting for a considerable number of dead Hun.

CASUALTIES
9th February

Personnel	Killed	Wounded
Officers	—	Lt. Robinson ('C' Sqn)
Other Ranks	—	1
Total since 8 February	—	2 Offrs & 7 Other Ranks

Tanks	Mined	Penetrated Ap/Bazooka/Heavy HE
	1	—
Total sinces 8 February	3	—

10th February

At first light two troops of 'B' Squadron under command of Squadron Second-in-Command, moved down the causeway and joined 5/7th Gordons in the MILSBEEK area 772 486 for an attack on OTTERSUM, which was successful, and a small bridgehead was also obtained over the GENNEP bridge at 778 464. Later in the day the remainder of the Squadron moved to MILSBEEK. This Squadron now consisted of Squadron Headquarters, 2 Troops of 3 and 1 Troop of 2 Tanks which was left out of battle. The remaining tanks being casualties from being struck by mines the previous day and one troop with 'A' Squadron. In the centre one troop of 'C' Squadron reinforced by one troop of 'A' Squadron and one troop of 'B' Squadron proceeded to push on into the REICHSWALD in support of 5 Camerons (152 Brigade). Progress was slow owing to stiff enemy resistance and enemy SP or Anti tank guns being encountered, firing down the main road running North West, South East in this area. On the left one troop with 7th Argyll & Sutherland Highlanders (154 Brigade) pushed out patrols forward, but made no set piece attack since the main thrust, and all artillery support was centrea on the 152 Brigade front in the centre. The 'A' Squadron troop under command 'C' Squadron was brought across from the Northern to the centre thrust line, but in doing so two tanks were lost on mines and the third tank was used to complete the one troop of 'C' Squadron, which had lost one tank knocked out by an SP anti tank gun.

CASUALTIES
10th February

Personnel	Killed	Wounded
Officers	—	—
Other Ranks	1	1
Total since 8 February	1 other rank	2 Offrs & 8 ORs

Tanks	Mined	Penetrated Ap/Bazooka/Heavy HE
	1	—
	—	1 — 75 AP
Total since 8 February	—	1 — 75 AP

11th February

During the night of 10/11 February, 153 Brigade expanded its bridgehead into GENNEP and a class 40 Bailey Bridge was constructed over the River under shall and spandau fire. As soon as this was completed 'B' Squadron passed over the bridge and completed the mopping up of GENNEP and supported strong infantry thrusts south on the main road South of the railway, harbouring for the night area 783 454.

'C' Squadron still composed of only two troops, one from 'B' Squadron and the other consisting of two tanks from 'C' Squadron and one tank from 'A' Squadron, continued to support 152 Brigade, a troop with each forward battalion, 2nd and 5th Seaforths. An attack down the main road to HEKKENS 833 481 was held up by mines and an anti tank ditch and was eventually withdrawn. In the evening 154 Brigade was put through 152 Brigade, right 7 Black Watch with in support one troop 'A' Squadron — task, capture HEKKENS; left 1 Black Watch with in support one troop 'A' Squadron — task, capture NERGENA 8347. Both attacks were successful and many prisoners of war were taken.

CASUALTIES
11th February

Personnel	Killed	Wounded
Officers	—	—
Other Ranks	1	1
Total since 8 February	1 other rank	2 Offrs & 9 ORs

	Tanks	Mined	Penetrated Ap/Bazooka/Heavy HE
		1	1 Heavy HE
Total since 8 February	4		2

12th February

153 Brigade continued to push south and south east from GENNEP and 'B' Squadron was reinforced by one troop of 'C' Squadron. On the right 1st Gordons supported by one troop of 'C' Squadron under commend 'B' Squadron, secured HEYEN 7843. On the left 5/7th Gordons supported by two troops of 'B' Squadron secured HEIDE 8045 and Pt 24.3 (797 447). 'B' Squadron harboured for the night in the area 785 454. There was heavy shelling of this area during the night.

The two troops of 'A' Squadron in support of 7th and 1st Black Watch respectively remained with these battalions during the night 11/12 February and throughout 12th February in a counter attack role.

The two troops of 'C' Squadron remained with their respective forward battlions of 152 Brigade but had no tasks to perform.

CASUALTIES
Nil

13th February

153 Brigade remained in positions secured on 12th February. On the right one troop from 'C' Squadron under command 'B' Squadron remained in support 1st Gordons in the area HEYEN. On the left one troop 'B' Squadron remained in support 5/7th Gordons. During the afternoon the enemy launched a counter attack on point 24.3 (797 447). This attack was supported by enemy SP anti tank guns.

The Troop Leader of the troop of tanks supporting 5/7th Gordons was unfortunately killed by HE whilst carrying out a reconnaissance on foot preparatory to dealing with this attack. The main weight of this counter attack was felt on the right sector, where in shocking visibility the 'C' Squadron. Troop remained within 300 yards of the enemy Armour for 2 hrs after darkness to produce a break through. The attack however, was successfully beaten off.

154 Brigade continued to push south from the area HEKENS—NERGENA to the line of the River NIERS. 'A' Squadron protected the left flank by firing an indirect shoot on to KESSEL (MR 8546).

One troop only of 'C' Squadron remained with the forward troops of 152 Brigade, remainder were withdrawn to Squadron Headquarters as there was no task for them.

CASUALTIES
13th February

Personnel	Killed	Wounded
Officers	Lt. Walker ('B' Sqn)	—
Others Ranks	—	—
Total since 8 February	1 Offr & 1 OR	2 Offrs & 9 ORs

Tanks	Mined	Penetrated Ap/Bazooka/Heavy HE
	—	—
Total since 8 February	4	2

14th February

153 Brigade remained in areas secured on the 12th February. 'B' Squadron had one troop supporting each of the two forward battalions in a counter attack role.

During the night 14/15 February, 154 Brigade carried out an attack to secure a bridgehead south of the River NIERS. Before and during the attack a composite force of tanks commanded by Capt Hamber, Second-in-Command 'C' Squadron, and consisting of one troop from 'C' Squadron, one troop from 'B' Squadron, one troop from 'A' Squadron, and two 95 mm from 'A' Squadron Headquarters carried out a diversionary shoot on to KESSEL from the area of the houses at 842 477. Ammunition was to have dumped been for this shoot but owing to the bad condition of the road through the REICHSWALD it was imposible to get extra ammunition forward and the fire programme had to be curtailed more than half of the ammunition carried in the tanks being used. The diversion started at 2100 hrs and continued to 2345 hrs. The Squadron group harboured for the night in the area of Cross Roads 826 495.

15th February

On the 153 Brigade front the 3th Black Watch supported by one troop of 'B' Squadron moved Sout East from HEYEN to secure the Cross tracks at 795 424.

The successful night attack of 154 Brigade enabled the road OTTERSUM 7846 HEKKENS to be opened. This made 'B' possible a re-grouping of troops within squadrons The 'B' Squadron Troop with 'C' Squadron returned to 'B' Squadron and the 'C' Squadron Troop with 'B' Squadron returned to 'C' Squadron. 'A' Squadron in support 154 Brigade moved across the River NIERS at GENNEP to VILLER (8346). Later one troop moved to the area TILE WORKS (8346) in support of 1 Black Watch and one troop joined 7 Argylls preparatory to the attack on KESSEL during the night 15/16 February.

Before 154 Brigade launched their attack on KESSEL, 'C' Squadron put down harrassing fire on the area KESSEL, from 2045 hrs to 2145 hrs. During this period 500 rounds of 75 mm and 120 rounds of 95 mm were fired. The ammunition for this shoot was successfully dumped during the afternoon. The shoot was fired from the same area as the prevvious night

CASUALTIES
Nil

16th February

153 Brigade. 1st Gordons with in support one Troop 'B' Squadron secured start line for 52 Division attack in the area 819 418.

154 Brigade. 1st Black Watch with in support 'A' Squadron's Headquarters and one Troop, one troop of Crocodiles, and one Troop of SP anti-tank gun, captured HASSUM Railway Station (845 447). One troop of 'A' Squadron remained in support 7th Argylls in the area KESSEL.

152 Brigade. 'C' Squadron had no tasks and carried out maintennance.

CASUALTIES
16th February

Personnel	Killed	Wounded
Officers	—	—
Other Ranks	—	—
Total since 8 February	1 Offr & 1 Other Rank	2 Offr & 10 Other Ranks
Tanks	Mined	Penetrated Ap/Bazooka/Heavy HE
	—	—
Total since 8 February	4	2

17th February

153 Brigade. Throughout the day 'B' Squadron remained in reserve in the area 785 454. Squadron Leader attended planning conferences for attack on GOCH.

154 Brigade. At first light one troop of 'A' Squadron moved forward in support of one Company 7th Argylls to clear enemy pockets of resistance East of KESSEL. 75 prisoners of War were taken. One other troop remained in the area KESSEL in support of 7th Argylls less one company. During the morning this Troop had one officer and four other ranks wounded by enemy mortar fire. The remainder of 'A' Squadron was concentrated in the area VILLER.

152 Brigade. No tasks for 'C' Squadron. 'C' Squadron remained concentrated throughout the day in KESSEL. With the opening of the road between OTTERSUM and HEKKENS it had been possible to bring forward the remaining two troops of 'C' Squadron from the original concentration area on D-Day. Owing to the state of the roads through the REICHSWALD these troops had to be left out of battle until the main road could be used.

CASUALTIES

17th February

Personnel	Killed	Wounded
Officers	—	Lt. Lander 'A' Sqn
Other Ranks	—	4
Total since 8 February	1 Offr & 1 Other Rank	3 Offrs & 14 Other Ranks
Tanks	Mined	Penetrated Ap/Bazooka/Heavy HE
	—	—
Total since 8 February	4	2

18th February

152 Brigade. No tasks for 'C' Squadron. 'C' Squadron remained THAL (8746) and continued planning for attack on GOCH.

154 Brigade. 'A' Squadron remained concentrated in reserve in the area of VILLER.

152 Brigade. During the night of 18/19 February this Brigade carried out a night attack on the outer defences of the West side of GOCH. During the hours of daylight 18th February 'C' Squadron moved from their concentration area near HEKKENS over the River NIERS by the Cl. 40 bridge at GENNEP to the area of woods 826 467. Half of a Squadron of Crocodiles, one Troop A.V.R.E.'s, and one troop Flails, joined the Squadron at OTTERSUM, before crossing the GENNEP bridge. The Squadron was to be prepared to support 152 Brigade at first light 19th February.

CASUALTIES
Nil

19th February

152 Brigade. At first light Troops of 'C' Squadron joined Battalions as follows: — One Troop — 2 Seathforths, area wood 867 458. One Troop — 5 Seathforths, area ASPERDEN 8845. One Troop 5 Camerons area HERVORST 8946. During the night this Brigade had secured all objectives but a number of pillboxes had been bypassed and had still to be cleared up. The Troop (Lt. Thorogood) with 5 Camerons carried out a very successful action aginst pillboxes during the day with A.V.R.E.'s and Crocodiles in support. Many prisoners of War were taken.

Procedure for clearing the pillboxes was as follows: — Having isolated the pillbox with smoke a round of 75 HE was fired at the back door or one of the embrasures. On some occasions this was quite sufficient to produce a white flag. If, however the desired effect was not produced by firing this round, one tank A.V.R.E. was brought up within range and fired its petard until the door or embrasure was burst open. If the Hun continued to be obstinate a squirt of fire from the Crocodiles, either silenced the pillbox for good or produced immediate surrender.

154 Brigade. 'A' Squadron remained concentrated in reserve in the area of VILLER as a firm base. 154 Brigade resting as many troops as possible.

153 Brigade. As soon as 152 Brigade secured their objective this Brigade was passed through to take the area of GOCH South of the River NIERS. The 5th Black Watch and the 5/7 Gordons with in support of each one Troop of 'B' Squadron entered the town at first light. The 1st Gordons with in support one Troop 'B' Squadron began clearing the outskirts. During the fierce house to house fighting Lieut. Jackson was killed

when a bazooka fired from a nearby house struck and entered the turret of his tank.

CASUALTIES
19th February

Personnel	Killed	Wounded
Officers	Lt. Jackson ('B')	Lt. Ward ('B' Sqn)
Other Ranks	—	2
Total since 8 February	2 Offrs & 1 OR	4 Offrs & 16 ORs

Tanks	Mined	Penetrated Ap/Bazooka/Heavy HE
	—	1 Bazooka-d
Total since 8 February	4	3
Attd Vehs	1 Crocodile Mined	

20th February

152 Brigade. Tank Troops remained with their respective battalions during the night 19/20 February. The troop with 2 Seaforths was withdrawn during daylight to Squadron HQ at GRAFENTHAL. The Brigade remained inactive throughout the day forming a firm base and resting as many troops a possible. 154 Brigade. 7 Black Watch with in support one Troop 'A' Squadron moved to area GOCH at first light and came under command 153 Brigade. 'A' Squadron less one troop remained area VILLER in reserve.

153 Brigade. 1 Gordons with in support one Troop 'B Squadron captured the area houses 899 421. 5/7 Gordons with in support one Troop 'B' Squadron remained in position secured on the 19th February. Remainder of 'B' Squadron were harboured in the area GRAFENTHAL. In order to rest 'B' Squadron as much as possible one Troop of 'C' Squadron were placed under command 'B' Squadron in case a fourth Troop should be required in the town but this was found unnecessary and this Troop was not employed.

CASUALTIES
Nil

21st February

152 Brigade. Two Troops of 'C' Squadron continued clearing up the pillboxes in the area West of the outer defences of GOCH resturning to the Squadron harbour area at GRAFEN-THAL in the evening. 170 prisoners of War were taken.

153 Brigade. One Troop of 'B Squadron remained with one Troop of SP Anti-tank guns in a counter attack role in support of 5 Black Watch in the area THOMASHOF (899 421). One tank from this Troop was lost on a mine. The troop from 'A' Squadron under command of 'B' Squadron supporting the 7 Black Watch in their attack to secure the factory at 910 426.

154 Brigade. The Brigade moved to area GOCH. 7 Black Watch with in support one Troop 'A' Squadron reverted to command 154 Brigade and continued its clearing task in GOCH. 7 Argylls with in support one troop of 'A' Squadron moved to the east end of GOCH. The remainder of 'A' Squadron concentrated in the area 899 436.

One light tank was damaged by a mine whilst assisting C. R. A. 51 (H) Division in reconnaissance of new gun area.

CASUALTIES
21st February

Personnel	Killed	Wounded
Officers	—	—
Other Ranks	—	1
Total since 8 February	2 Offrs & 1 Other Rank	4 Offrs & 17 Other Ranks

Tanks	Mined	Penetrated Ap/Bazooka/Heavy HE
	2	1 - shell
Total since 8 February	6	4

22nd February

152 Brigade. One Troop 'C' Squadron (LT. SPRATT) with 5 Seaforths cleared two pillboxes during the day.

154 Brigade. One Troop 'A' Squadron in counter-attack role in support of 7 Black Watch, remainder of Squadron concentrated in area 899 436. During the day the Squadron was shelled and had five other ranks wounded.

153 Brigade. 'B' Squadron in reserve in the area GRAFEN-THAL.

CASUALTIES

22nd February

Personnel	Killed	Wounded
Officers	—	—
Other Ranks	—	—
Total since 8 February	2 Offrs & 1 Other Ranks	4 Offrs & 22 Other Ranks
Tanks	Mined	Penetrated Ap/Bazooka/Heavy HE
	—	—
Total since 8 February	6	4

23rd February

152 Brigade. Capt. Hamber, Second-in-Command 'C' Squadron and one troop moved off to clear a further two pillboxes but as no A.V.R.E. tanks were available this operation was cancelled.
154 Brigade. One troop 'A' Squadron remained in support of 7 Black Watch in a counter attack role. Remainder of Squadron still concentrated in area 899 436.
153 Brigade. 'B' Squadron remained in reserve area GRAFENTHAL.

CASUALTIES

Nil

24th February

All Squadrons in reserve in Squadron areas.

CASUALTIES

Nil

25th February

152 Brigade. It was decided to carry out a night attack 25/26 February with Camerons to secure BOECKELT 8842. As a diversion. 'C' Squadron were to carry out harrassing fire on SIEBENGEWALD 8741 during the attack. The harassing force was commanded by Lieut. McMartin of 'C' Squadron and was composed of three troops from 'C' Squadron and one 95 mm and two 75 mm tanks from R.H.Q. Ammunition was dumped during the afternoon and the shoot was a great success. Du-

ring the night Capt. Hamber, Second-in-Command 'C' Squadron, with under command one troop 'B' Squadron half Squadron Crocodiles, and one troop A.V.R.E.'s, concentrated in the area 5 Camerons 885 445 ready to assist as required at first light 26th February.

154 Brigade. 'A' Squadron still concentrated in area 899 436. During the night 25/26 February an ammunition truck from a maintenance train of 53 Division artillery was hit and set on fire by shelling, and members of 'A' Squadron assisted in driving and towing eight vehicles away from the area of exploding ammunition. The vehicles had been abandoned by the RASC and artillery personnel.

153 Brigade. 'B' Squadron remained concentrated in area GRAFENTHAL.

CASUALTIES
Nil

26th February

152 Brigade. 5 Camerons night attack was very successful and 'C' Squadron was not asked to give support until 0830 hrs when one troop supported 'C' Company 5 Camerons in mopping up. 30 Prisoners of War were taken without a round being fired. During the night 26/27 February, remaining Battalions of 152 Brigade attacked SIEBENGEWALD but were held up by determined resistance in the neck of the loop of the River KENDEL at 8642.

153 Brigade. 5/7 Gordons were held in readiness to attack the Seminary 8840 and Customs House 8740. 'B' Squadron was to be prepared to support this attack. This attack however, was not put in until the 27th February.

154 Brigade. During the night 26/27 February 7 Argylls with in support one troop of 'A' Squadron attacked and captured HUIM 9040 and KERKENHOF 8939. This troop lost one tank on a mine. 7 Black Watch with in support one Troop 'A' Squadron secured BOYENHOF 8839. One Troop 'A' Squadron was held in reserve area HULM.

CASUALTIES
26th February

Personnel	Killed	Wounded
Officers	—	—
Other Ranks	—	—
Total since 8 February	2 Offrs & 1 Other Rank	4 Offrs & 22 Other Ranks

Tanks	Mined	Penetrated Ap/Bazooka/Heavy HE
	1	—
Total since 8 February	7	4

27th February

152 Brigade. Owing to stiff resistance encountered during the night attack, a force consisting of two Troops 'C' Squadron, one Troop Avres, one Troop Crocodiles, under command Capt. Hamber, Second-in-Command 'C' Squadron, was concentrated by 0600 hrs in area North of HASSUM 8543, prepared for action at first light. By first light, however, resistance had been overcome and this force was not required. 'C' Squadron concentrated at GRAFENTHAL by 1700 hrs.

153 Brigade. 5/7 Gordons supported by one troop 'B' Squadron captured the Seminary and Customs House.

154 Brigade. By 2345 hrs 'A' Squadron was concentrated in reserve in the area 899 436.

CASUALTIES
Nil

28th February

51 (H) Division resting. 'A' Squadron concentrated area VILLER for rest period. 'B' and 'C' Squadrons restingg area GRAFENTHAL.

CASUALTIES

28th February		
Personnel	Killed	Wounded
Officers	—	—
Other Ranks	—	—
Total since 8 February	2 Offrs & 1 Other Rank	4 Offrs & 22 Other Ranks

Tanks	Mined	Penetrated Ap/Bazooka/Heavy HE
	—	—
Total since 8 February	7	4
Total attached vehicles since 8 February	1 Croc Tank 1 SP A/Tk Gun	and brewed up 1 Flail bazookoed
Total All Vehicles since 8 February	9	5

LESSONS LEARNT FROM OPERATIONS COVERING THE PERIOD 8th—28th FEBRUARY 1945

1. Pillboxes

(a) These reinforced concrete fortifications were found to consist of three embrasures sited to cover together 360^0. Each embrasure was made of steel $3^1/_2''$ to $4''$ thick mounted in concrete approx 2 ft thick. Behind each one was a concrete room with a steel door leading into a passage connecting each embrasure with the other two and with sleeping quarters in the centre of the pillbox. Each room contained a Spandau machine gun on a mounting sited to fire through an opening in the centre of the embrasure. The outside walls and roof of the pillbox were covered with earth and grass sods for protection and concealment. At the side of the embrasures at the rear of the pillbox was the entrance, protected by an open steel gate. A belt of trip wire and mines circled each pillbox in a radius of approx 50—80 yards. Pillboxes were sited to support each other and were between 800—1000 yards apart. Each pair of pillboxes appeared to be controlled from a pillbox sited between them. This pillbox was purely for control and had no embrasures.

(b) Method of Attack.
    (i) Isolation of the pillbox. Smoke is put down either by artillery or 95 mm of Squadron HQ on the flanks and rear of the pillbox to ensure that the attacking force is provided with complete defilade from the flanks.
    (ii) 75 mm HE is fired at one of the embrasures by the Troop of tanks. Sometimes this was sufficient to produce a white flag and the occupants surrendered. If, however, they were made of tougher material, the reply was usally a burst of machine gun fire.
    (iii) Covered by the tank Troop an A.V.R.E. tank moved up to within Petard range and proceded to blast open the embrasure. Sometimes this was sufficient to produce surrender, if not.
    (iv) A Crocodile tank was brought forward and squirted flame into the gaping hole. The blast from the petard sometimes burst open the inside door of the room thus

enabling the flame to reach right inside the pillbox. The result was either to burn the occupants or to produce their immediate surrender to the waiting infantry.

(d) Squirting flame without first breaking open the pillbox with a petard was found to be of little value. As soon/as the Spandau gunner saw the Crocodile approaching, all he had to do was dismount his gun and retire behind his door into the inner chamber of the pillbox and wait for the flaming to cease. The blast from the petard described above, burst open this door enabling the flame to reach right inside.

(e) No anti tank guns were found in these pillboxes. All anti tank guns appeared to be sited in open earthwork positions covering the approaches to the pillboxes. During the attack on the pillbox they were, therefore, easily neutralised by smoke or artillery fire. If, however, an anti tank gun had been mounted alongside each Spandau the task of dealing with the pillbox would have been far more hazardous.

2. Employment of Single Tank Troops

Throughout this operation single troops were constantly being employed to support. Battalion or Company attacks. The troop moved in rear of the leading infantry and dealt with opposition holding them up. Communications were provided between the Infantry and Tank Troop by having the Squadron Leader or a Liaison Officer at Brigade or Battalion Headquarters in a light tank or another Churchill tank from the Squadron. The Squadron Leader or Liaison Officer kept the troop in the general infantry picture, the remaining information was obtained by direct observation of the infantry movement by the Troop Leader coupled with an inquisitive mind, initiative, and courage to dismount under fire, if necessary, and to ask what was holding the infantry up, at the same time a little plan was made with the infantry commander on the spot to deal with the trouble. With smoke, HE and AP, a troop should, and is capable of looking after itself provided it remembers the old rule of Fire and Movement.

3. Use of Tanks by night in artificial Moonlight

One Troop supported a night attack throughout the whole attack dealing successfully with several Spandau positions. The Troop Leader stated that the light provided by the searchlights was sufficient to enable him to 'hosepipe' his Besas assisted by tracer. He could not see to fire accurately through his telescope. As in day attacks the troop moved in rear of forward infantry and was only brought forward when there was a definite task, and was not launched until a plan had been made between the Troop Leader and infantry Commander on the spot to deal with the opposition holding up the advance.

4. Early Planning and early Orders

Throughout this operation, in spite of the almost continual fighting, all planning for next day's fighting was done early in the day, as a result, Orders with a few exceptions which could not be avoided, were issued early and the fighting troops were able to got a reasonable night's rest, this combined with the practice of having a proportion of troops left out of battle each day, and the Squadron Second-in-Command answering at times for the Squadron Leader, undoubtedly enabled troops to continue fighting over this long period without undue strain.

5. Street Fighting.

(a) Tanks must support infantry from behind and shoot them into the houses which the latter are going to clear.

To put tanks in front of infantry will only result in casualties from enemy Bazookas, hidden in ground and first floors of neighbouring houses, with the consequent loss of tank support. Tanks within the Troop must at all times be mutually supporting covering windows of houses on either side of the road. The only tank casualties from Bazooka-ing in the severe street fighting in GOCH was when a troop Leader went forward with his tank alone to support infantry.

(b) Crocodiles if used for house clearance must have room for manoeuvre, and there must be room for them to be given fire support by tanks of the Armoured Regiment.

Accordingly they are only of value in towns which have wide roads and open squares, and only when such roads are not partly blocked by rubble. In GOCH the roads in the town were too narrow to employ Crocodiles and the were used on the outskirts against known hardcores of enemy resistance.

PERSONAL MESSAGE FROM THE COMMANDER 51st HIGHLAND DIVISION

The following letter reached me today from Lieut.-General B. G. Horrocks, CB, DSO, M.C., Commanding 30 Corps: —

"I have seen the 51st Highland Division fight many battles since I met them just before ALAMAIN. But I am certain that the Division has never fought better than in the recent offensive into Germany.
You breached the enemy's defences in the initial attack, fought your way through the Southern part of the REICHSWALD, overcame in succession several strong points of the Siegfried Line such as HEKKENS, etc., and then finally cleared the Southern half of GOCH — a key centre in the German defences.
You have accomplished everything that you have been asked to do in spite of the number of additional German reserves which have been thrown in on your front. No Division has ever been asked to do more and no Division has ever accomplished more.
Well done, the Highland Division".

I am sure the operations of the Division which culminated in the capture of the Siegfried Bastion of GOCH will go down in history as one of the finest achievements of the Fifty-First. Although the brunt of the fighting has necessarily been borne by the infantry who were magnificent, success was only made possible by the great co-operation of all Arms and by the determined effort of every single man in the Division to give of his best.
I thank every one of you for what you have done towards the destruction of the German Army.
There may be tough times ahead but the end is at last clearly in sight.
Good luck to you all.
BLA.   (sgd)   J. S. Rennie,
24 Feb 45.   Major General.

NOTES — 1. This message of course includes 107 Regt Royal Armoured Corps, The Scottish Horse, 'A' Squadron 1 Fife and Forfor Yeomanry, 'B' Squadron 1 Lothian and Border Horse, and the 222 Assault Sqn A.R.E., who formed a part of the Highland Division for these operations.

2. Divisional Casualties for the operation were: —

Killed		Wounded		Missing	
Offrs	ORs	Offrs	ORs	Offrs	ORs
23	183	80	997	3	141

Our prisoners totalled 53 Officers and 2695 Other Ranks and a great number of Germans were killed.

Conclusion.

I had hoped to be able to write a Part II to this little history recording the Regiment's service in the closing stages of the JAPANESE WAR. But that was not to be as I briefly relate below.

While concentrated MUNSTER, we learnt our orders in June 1945. We were to go to SEAC as a Tank Btn (light) together with other units of an old Bde, the 34th Armoured Bde. To prepare us for the new theatre much reorganization was necessary, and we lost some 300 officers and men of early release groups, taking in in their place an equivalent number by rank and trade from the 147 Regiment R.A.C., a converted of the Hampshire Regiment. B Sqn became "Hampshire Sqn" under Major J. A. H. Box, and the remainder of the Hampshire intake were distributed throughout the rest of the Regt.

Lt. Col. H. H. K. Rowe, now awarded the DSo, left us at this time to take command of the Rhine Army R.A.C. Trg Regt. Lt. Col. R. H. Taite, who had been one of the original Coy Comdrs in the Regt. when it was the 50th Holding Btn King's Own, in 1940 and again Coy Comdr and Regtl 2 i/c of the 10th Btn and 2 i/c of the Regt when re-named 151 Regt R.A.C. on conversion in 1942, was posted and assumed command. Many of the old King's Own officers and OR's accompanied Lt. Col. Rowe to his new command, and there have found a happy home for the last few months of their Army service.

For a short while training in normal tank warfare went on apace with special training based on lessons already learnt in the Far Eastern Theatre, together with the usual training in precautions against tropical diseases and malaria. Never had a Regt possessed such magnificent material, with practically every man trade tested and mustered in one or more trades and battle experienced to boot. The average age, including the C. O, Q. M, W. O'S and senior ranks was 24 years.

But our enthusiasm for battle was short lived. The Atom Bomb caused the sudden collapse of JAPAN and diverted our thoughts and energies towards peace and civil life. A few weeks of uncertainty ended in the new decision that we would not sail for SEAC but would remain in BAOR as an "unbased" armd regt on occupational "equivalent btn". Our tanks were removed from us and we became in effect "black-hatted infantry".

I will not bore you with any long description of a life as an occupational unit or of our duties thus taken on. Sufficient to say that all commitments given to us were faithfully performed but that most of our energies were turned towards sport and physical fitness, welfare and entertainments, preparation and education for civil life. During August we had to decentralize with H.Q. and A Sqns in MUNSTER, B Spn out at EVERSWINKEL and C Spn out at BILLERBECK. At the end of September we moved again and established ourselves with H. Q. at LAGGENBECK near OSNABRÜCK and A, B and C Sqns at LENGERICH.

In October 1945 another reorganization, on the reverse principle, was carried out. Again some 300 officers and men, this time of late release groups, left us to keep going the regular units of the 7th Armd Div. In replacement we received N.C.O's and men of the earlier release groups from those same units, namely 5th Royal Inniskilling Dragoon Guards, 8th King's Royal Irish Hussars, 1st Royal Tank Regiment and 5th Royal Tank Regiment. Later also we received other small drafts from the 4/7th Dragoon Guards, 1st Fife and Forfar Yeomanry 4th Royal Tank Regiment, 9th Royal Tank Regiment, 11th Royal Tank Regiment, and the 49th Armoured Personnel Carrier Regiment. Very few men now remain of those originally enlisted with the King's Own prior to conversion to R.A.C. in 1942.

In October also the "King's Own College" opened in LENGERICH under the guidance of Maj B. H. Wilson MBE and Capt C. H. Deakin MC. Some 20 different subjects were offered to the men and some 450 men availed themselves of the offer. Excellent results were obtained.

Early in 1946 the reorganization of the Army of Occupation, due to the release programme and the final settlement of what forces are to remain in Germany, caused a considerable move round among units of the Bde. We have been lucky in that this has only meant the move of C Sqn from LENGERICH to WESTERKAPPELN. But we ourselves in the throes of preparing for final disbandment or "suspended animation" (we don't know which yet) and by the end of February 1946 the 107 Regt R.A.C. (King's Own) will have passed into the pages of history.

As an Epitaph I would to conclude with these remarks. Thanks to a good start made under Lt. Col. Crow's command, this regt (a battalion — call what it what you will) has been well known throughout for its smartness of discipline and turnout, its military efficiency, and the friendly spirit of comradeship to be found throughout all ranks. Despite its present diluted state of officers and men and despite intakes of be-medalled veterans of many other regiments, it has retained to the end very noticeably its identity as a unit, and, though doubtless with a few pangs of regret here and there, disperses to civil life and other units "clean, sober and properly dressed".

HONOURS AND AWARDS

The following personnel of the Regt were awarded decorations in the Field.

D. S. O.
    Lt. Col. H. H K. Rowe   (41 463)

M. C.
    Major D. H. Davies   (77 603)
    Capt. M. O. Caton   (129 315)
    Capt. W. R. F. Cockcroft   (138 700)
    Major E. C. Garner   (137 394)
    Lt. J. H. Walker   (315 901)*
    Lt. J. S. McMartin   (232 545)
    Capt. D. J. Phillips   (258 214)
    Lt. D. C. H. Sutherland   (145 084)

M. B. E.
    Capt. B. H. Wilson   (174 963)

Croix de Guerre — Silver Star
    Lt. M. L. A. Hill   (268 009)
    Lt. I. F. E. Myers   (276 102)

Croix de Guerre — Palm
    3 703 694 Sgt. Rowlandson E.

D. C. M.
    3 715 768 Tpr. Piper R.

M. M.
    7 945 125 Cpl. Brooker D. W.
    6 028 289 Cpl. Newall J. D.
    3 065 119 Tpr. Foster R.
    7 893 530 Sgt. MacLean E. A.
    7 656 662 Sgt. Jolley J. B. (R. E. M. E.)
       97 781 Sgt. Darke J. R. (R. E. M. E.)
    1 506 357 Sgt. Symonds E. W. (R. E. M. E.)
    3 716 283 Sgt. Corker W.
    3 382 809 W/Cpl. Taylor W.

Croix de Guerre — Bronze Star
    3 715 772 L/Cpl. Garner E.

---

* Since killed in action.

HONOURS AND AWARDS — CITATIONS

Lt. Col. H. H. K. ROWE

Citation for D.S.O.

Lt. Col. H. H. K. ROWE commanded a detached Churchill Tank Regiment with conspicuous success during the operation "VERITABLE" particularly from Ferbuary 8th to 27th 1945. His Regiment fought an almost continuous series of small actions under the command of 51 (H) Div. and in support at various times of all Infantry Brigades and every Battalion in the Division. This entailed the widest variety of Infantry-Tank actions by day and night and ranged from thick forest fighting to overcoming bunkers and very large concrete fortified works in the open plain.

All Squadron organisation in the unit was disrupted during several periods and for days at a time and the outstanding energy displayed and personal grip on all ranks in his Regiment exercised by this Commanding Officer throughout the long period of strain has received the highest and unqualified praise from the Infantry of this Division, for the most completely successful co-operation and support given to them throughout the period.

Military Cross

Major D. H. Davies (77 603)

At first light on the morning 8th August 1944, Major Davies' Squadron was ordered over the crossing over the River ORNE at BRIEUX to protect the bridge at all costs. He led his Squadron forward through heavy shellfire and mines and in face of attack by enemy Panther tanks. Although he lost 5 tanks on mines he eventually led the remainder of his Squadron forward and fought the enemy tanks throughout the day. His own tank was hit and set on fire. In spite of flames and Spandau fire directed on his tank he personally rescued his wounded operator from the turret and returned to remove the body of his dead gunner but was finally driven off by enemy spandau fire and the intensity of the flames.

When only two tanks of his Squadron were left he came back on foot to report to his C. O., then returned also on foot to stay with the Infantry whom he was supporting, where he remained watching the actions of his two tanks until ordered to withdraw by Second-in-Command of the Brigade at about 2230 hrs on 9th August.

Throughout a long and trying period, without sleep and with little food, he displayed the utmost gallantry, efficiency, vigour and cheerfulness, and his personal example did much to maintain the morale of both the Infantry and his own Regiment in a most difficult and critical situation. No praise is high enough for the conduct of this young offficer.

Capt. M. O. Caton (129 315)

On 7th August 1944, Capt. Caton was Squadron Reconnaissance Officer of 'A' Squadron 107 Regt., R. A. C. which was providing flank protection for the bridgehead across the River ORNE (9551) established by 59 Infantry Division.

During the evening the enemy launched a determined counterattack by TIGER and PANTHER tanks. There was little room for manoeuvre to the S. E. of the bridgehead and 'A' Squadron was soon virtually isolated from the bridge and infantry support. Out of wireless touch and by this time without Squadron Leader, Capt. Caton re-established contact by making his way on foot to the bridge, regardless of the heavy mortar and small arms fire he encountered. Finding that the bridge was unprotected from the EAST, Capt. Caton assisted in organising an infantry company to perform the task. Four times during the night Capt. Caton made his way under heavy and continuous enemy fire between his tanks and the bridge; tirelessly organising defences and guiding reinforcement tanks forward; entirely without concern for his personal safety. He took over the Squadron and arranged tank support for three infantry battalions in the bridgehead.

During the day of 8th August, Capt. Caton was commanding 10 of the 13 tanks still alive in the bridgehead and during the afternoon laid on an attack against three PANTHERS and two TIGERS in the village of BRIEUX; he forced these to withdrawn, captured 4 prisoners of war and evacuated several of our own wounded infantry.

Throughout the fierce enemy counter-attacks against our bridgehead, Capt. Caton showed great determination and initiative; his leadership was an inspiration during this precarious period and there can be no doubt that his fighting spirit communicated itself to his men.

Capt. W. R. F. Cockroft (138 700)

During 7/8 August, 107 R. A. C. were in support of the infantry of 59 Infantry Division in the bridgehead across the River ORNE (9551). On the late evening of 7th August, when communications had broken down, Capt. Cockroft accompanied his Squadron Leader through enemy positions, passing through heavy LMG and mortar fire, to regain contact witch 'C' Squadron tanks on the left of the bridgehead.

Later, and still under enemy fire, he rescued a wounded trooper from a knocked-out tank and evacuated him across the river. At 0500 hrs, 8th August, when reinforcement tanks ran on to a minefield, Capt. Cockroft went forward, and, ignoring enemy mortar fire an sniping assisted his Squadron Leader in locating and lifting the mines, thereby permitting the tanks to move up in close support to the infantry.

Later in the morning he was slightly wounded in the leg by a mortar splinter but refused to be evacuated.

By contacting 'C' Squadron, night 7th August, Capt. Cockroft did much to co-ordinate and strengthen resistance to enemy armour; throughout the action this courageous Officer showed a tireless devotion to duty and a calm disregard for personal safety that was an inspiration to all ranks.

Major E. C. Garner (137 394)

During the period 20—29 October 1944 ,Major Garner, Commander 'C' Squadron 107 Regt., R. A. C., was in action seven days during the operation to cut the BERGEN—OP—ZOOM—ROSENDAAL ROAD.

During these actions, which varied from village clearing with infantry, to tank actions against enemy S. P. gun positions in open country, he commanded his Squadron with coolness, courage, and determination.

On 27th October, whilst his Squadron was advancing across country to seize BREMBOSCH, his tank was knocked out by a direct hit from an enemy 75 mm SP. at a range of approx 700 yards. The A. P. shell killed his co-driver and wounded his operator.

Major Garner remained in his tank under SP. fire to control his Squadron while smoke was put down and his tank towed under cover. He then ordered his Squadron Second-in-Command to take over command of the Squadron while he changed tanks. He then evacuated his crew under enemy small arms fire and having seen to the safety of his wounded operator mounted another tank and resumed control of his Squadron.

Throughout this and subsequent actions in the same operation Major Garner's ppersonal coolness and courage in the face of enemy fire was a fine example to his Squadron, and without doubt the excellent fighting qualities of this Squadron are attributable very largely to this Officer's personal example.

Lieut. J. H. Walker (315 901) — (Since killed in action)

On 8th February 1945, 'B' Squadron 107 R. A. C., was in support of 7 Black Watch during the attack by 154 Brigade, 51 (H) Division to seize BRUUK (770 526) and BREEDEWEG (766 523). Lieut. Walker's tank Troop was ordered forward to give close support to the Company of the Black Watch, who were trying to force a crossing of the anti-tank obstacle (767 527). Opposition was severe from enemy snipers and spandau teams in house adjacent to the obstacle, and the infantry Company Commander and Platoon Commander were killed Seeing this Lieut. Walker dismounted from his tank and took command temporarily of the infantry platoon in the area of his tank Troop and under his direction the attack continued to be pressed home supported by the fire of his troop of tanks.

In the afternoon of the same day, Lieut. Walker was ordered forward to support a company of the 5/7 Gordons of 153 Brigade, into a fortified position on the edge of the REICHSWALD FOREST (773 517). This he did with the utmost determination. In such close country he had many times to get out of his tank, in the face of heavy enemy sniping and lead his tanks forward on foot so that they might support the infantry from the best positions. Long after it was too dark to see to fire his guns he remained with the infantry giving all the assistance of which he was capable.

Again on 12th February 1945, Lieut. Walker's Troop took part in the assault on the high ground south of GENNEP (7844). Here again he was indefatigable in his efforts to support the infantry, constantly dismounting from his tank and exposing himself to enemy fire in order to ensure complete liaison of his Troop with the infantry they were supporting.

This young officer's bravary, leadership, and devotion to duty in all the above instances were beyond praise and his name has become a bye-word among company officers in 153 Brigade.

Lieut. J. S. McMartin (232 545) (now Capt. McMartin)

Lieut. McMartin, commanding 4 Troop of 'C' Squadron 107 R.A.C., in the advance trough the REICHSWALD FOREST in support of 152 Brigade, 51 (H) Division, on 9, 10, and 11 February 1945.

During these three days Lieut. McMartin showed outstanding courage and devotion to duty. He commanded his Troop with great skill and through his own personal bravery instilled his crew into greater efforts to support the infantry through the wood.

During the first day he was wounded in the neck by enemy H.E. but refused to be evacuated.

On the second day his tank was fired at by an Anti-tank gun sited straight down the main track in the wood. Undaunted, realising that if he halted his tanks under cover the infantry would lose his support, he put down smoke in front of him and continued his advance, hoping to close with the anti-tank gun. The enemy anti-tank gun continued firing trough the smoke and knocked out his tank killing his co-driver. Lieut. McMartin immediately got into another tank and in co-operation with the infantry made a plan, disposed of the anti-tank gun, and continued the advance.

On the third day his tank ran on a mine breaking the track. Although under observed spandau and mortar fire, Lieut. McMartin dismounted from his tank, quickly repaired the track, with the assistance of the other members of the crew ,and continued to support his infantry.

During these three days this Officer, by his cheerfulness and willingness to undertake any task demanded of him by his infantry, was an inspiration to all around him. He showed complete disregard for his own personal safety and devotion to duty far above average.

Capt. D. J. Phillips. (258 214).

On 12th February 1945, 'B' Squadron 107 R.A.C., were in support of the 5/7 Gordons nad the 1st Gordons in an attack on the high ground south of GENNEP (7746).

Capt. Phillips was acting as liaison Officer between the troop of tanks supporting 1st Gordons in their attack on HEZELAND (7944) and the woods to the south.

At the commencement of the attack there was considerable artillery fire which was delaying the infantry, and quite undaunted Capt. Phillips continually dismounted from his tank and ran through enemy shell and spandau fire to ensure close liaison between the infantry and his tanks. Later, in the more open country ,the tanks at times got ahead of the infantry they were supporting and Capt. Phillips still continued to dismount from his tank and run over open ground, in spite of enemy aimed small arms fire, to contact his infantry and to find out how he could help them forward.

There is not the slightest doubt that had it not been for the untiring efforts of this gallant Officer ,the liaison between tanks and infantry would have broken down with the resultant increase in our own infantry casualties.

In addition to the above, this Officer has been Squadron Reconnaissance Officer for his Squadron in all actions since 8th February 1945, during the present operation.

He is outstandingly conscientious in his efforts to ensure close liaison between his tank Squadron and the Infantry with whom he is co-operating. His cheerfulness, bravery and determination to ensure the success of any operation which he may be ordered to carry out, are far above average, a fine example to other members of his Squadron, and promotes great confidence among the infantry whom he is supporting.

Periodical M. C.

    W S/L i e u t D. C. H. S u t h e r l a n d (145 084)

On the night of 26 February 1945, No 4 Troop, 'A' Squadron 107 R.A.C. was ordered forward in Searchlight "Movement Light" to support the attack of 7 Argyll & Sutherland Highlanders on HULM (903 405) and KEREENHOF (896 394) which had been temporarily held up by determined enemy machine gun fire in the HULM area.

In order to reach HULM it was necessary for Lieut Sutherland's troop to cross two anti tank obstacles which in the initial planning it had been decided that R. E.s would bridge to allow tanks to cross over.

The R. Es had not completed their task and warned Lt Sutherland not to proceed. However, he found a way over for his tanks, benefitting from the Movement Light and proceeded down the road to HULM well knowing that it had not been proved for anti tk mines. That there were mines on the verges Lieut. Sutherland knew well since an enemy mortar bomb exploded two mines when it fell in front of his tank just after he had crossed the first obstacles. Undeterred and realising that his early arrival at HULM was of vital importance to his infantry, Lieut. Sutherland led his troop into the village. There were no signs of his infantry there and although he was by now under constant enemy shell and mortar fire and knew the enemy were in close proximity he pushed on to the Southern edge of the village where he dismounted and after searching for some time he contacted the officer commanding the Coy which was held up. Having made a plan he proceeded to deal with enemy M. G. posts which were holding up his Infantry, by the tank Besa fire and crushing tactics.

All this was done in "Movement Light" over ground which Lieut. Sutherland had not seen in daylight, and in order to keep cantact with his Infantry in the semi darkness, he had to

continually dismount from his tank and run across open country under heavy arty, mortar and S. A. fire.
There is no doubt that it was only through the determination and perseverance oft his gallant Officer that his Infantry were able to gain their objectives with few casualties
During the numerous actions in operation "VERITABLE" from 8 to 27th Feb in which the 7 A & SH have taken part, Lieut. Sutherland has alway been asked for by name by the CO of that Bn for tank support, and nothing but the highest praise of his leadership and devotion to duty has been received from all infantry Officers with whom he has co-operated.

M. B. E.

C a p t. B. H. W i l s o n (174 963) — (N o w M a j o r)

Capt. Wilson has been Regimental Technical Adjutant of this Regiment for 19 months. He is quite tireless in his work and his devotion to duty is far above the average.
During the period 20—29 October 1944, this Regiment was in action every day except one. These continuous actions threw considerable strain on the mechanical fitness of the tanks since besides damage owing to enemy action, the ground over which such actions took place was at times very soft resulting in tanks becoming easily bogged.
At all times Capt. Wilson was well forward with his Armoured Recovery Vehicles, recovering tirelessly any damaged or broken down vehicles by day and night.
By the evening of 29 th October, after ten days advance and fighting, threequarters of the tank strength of the Regiment was still fit for action and every tank damaged by enemy fire, except one, had been recovered by Capt. Wilson to Base Workshop. This one exception was in HAINK village and attempts by Capt. Wilson to recover it on 29th October were driven off by A. P. and H. E. fire from enemy S. Ps. still holding out in the BULTENNEAR area.
The high standard of maintenance and tank fitness in the Regiment is largely due to Capt. Wilson's inexhaustable energy, unflagging keenness, and high sense of duty.

Croix-de Guerre — Silver Star

L i e u t. M. L. A. H i l l (268 009)

Prior to the attack of 107 R. A. C. and the Glasgow Highlanders on Saturday 15th July 1944, on the BON REPOS—ESQUAY area, the Regiment was formed up on the reverse slope of the

112 feature by Lieut. Hill. As well as this Regiment a troop of each — Crocodiles, A.V.R.E.S., and Flails, had to be included. Thus the Regiment had to start forming up at 1940 hrs for the 2145 zero. The F. U. P. was subjected to very severe mortar and artillery fire for the whole of this period, all tanks having to be completely closed down. Lieut. Hill, completely regardless of his own personal safety, formed the entire formation up himself on foot, which duty took him from 1930 hrs till 2115 hrs.

There is no doubt (in my mind) that the fact that the attack went in to time and under control was entirely due to the magnificient behaviour of this officer.

L i e u t. I. F E. M y e r s (Citation put in by Brigade)

Lieut. Myers fought with the Bde in France from 2 Jul 44 to the liberation of France. During this period he was employed as Liason Offr to Bde. HQ. He carried out his duties most faithfully never failing even when under intense enemy fire and despite difficult and dangerous conditions. He was twice wounded but quickly returned to duty.. On the last occasion when his scout car was blown up on a mine and the driver killed, despite personal wounds he walked four miles and got his message through.

This Offr displayed great devotion to duty and personal courage throughout the campaign in France.

His perseverance and gallantry have been an example to all.

Distinguished Conduct Medal

3 715 768 T p r. R. P i p e r (now L/C Piper)

On 21st October, during the attack on NIEUWMOER by 107 Regt., R. A. C., Tpr. Piper was co driver of the Troop Leader's tank of the leading tank Troops.

Enemy S. P. guns were known to be defending the village of NIEUWMOER, and on crossing the road running East and West through the village the Troop Leader's tank was engaged from close quarters by an enemy S. P. hidden amongst houses to the left rear.

The first round hit the tank and set the engine compartment on fire. Two more rounds followed in quick succession severely wounding the Troop Leader, Driver, and Gunner. The tank immediately caught fire.

Tpr. Piper evacuated his seat in the forward compartment of the tank and in spite of the danger from the burning tank

83

which might cause ammunition to explode at any moment, and the accurate enemy small arms fire directed at his tank from close range, he proceeded to lift his Troop Leader from the tank and drag him to safety.

He then returned to the tank which was still under enemy small arms fire and lifted the wounded Gunner from the Turret and dragged him to safety. The tank by now was burning fiercely and risk from exploding ammunition and petrol tanks was even greater than before.

In spite of this and the stream of enemy small arms fire which was by now continuously directed at his tank Tpr. Piper returned across the open ground for a third time and extracted the Driver and dragged him under cover.

He then rendered first aid to his Troop Leader, who was in danger of losing his life from loss of blood, and applied a tourniquet to his shattered leg. Next he applied first aid to the wounded driver, but on turning his attention to the Gunner he found that he had already died from wounds. He remained with them, still under small arms fire, until the enemy were driven back and his Troop Leader and Driver could be evacuated.

Tpr. Piper by his complete disregard for his own personal safety in returning repeatedly to his blazing tank whilst under accurate enemy fire undoubtedly saved the lives of his Tank Commander and Driver.

His gallant and unselfish conduct in most adverse circumstances is beyond praise.

Military Medal

7 945 125 C p l. B r o o k e r D. W. (n o w S g t. B r o o k e r)

On 7th August 1944, 12 Troop 'C' Squadron 107 Regt., R. A. C., was operating with 'B' Company 7th Norfolks in the area of GRIMBOSQ in the N. E. corner of the bridgehead across the River ORNE. At approximately 1300 hrs the enemy launched a heavy counter-attack against 'D' Company over running all the anti-tank guns and almost overwhelming the position. Two Tigers supported the attack and knocked out the Troop Leader's and Troop Sgt.'s tank, leaving Cpl. Brooker on his own. Cpl. Brooker managed to hit one of the Tigers and they withdrew. He then engaged and knocked out another Tiger which had moved up on the road to the West of GRIMBOSQ. After a number of their infantry had been killed, the enemy withdrew.

Undoubtedly the action of Cpl. Brooker, greatly assisted in breaking up the enemy's attack. Throughout the day Cpl. Brooker succeeded in breaking up several infantry counter-attacks by his machine gun fire.

By carrying on single handed as sole survivor of his troop against an enemy considerably superior in armour, Cpl. Brooker showed great courage and intiative.

6 028 289 C p l. N e w e l l J. D. (n o w L / S g t. N e w e l l)

This N. C. O. was, at 1330 hrs on 16 th July 1944, in action as Troop Leader's operator near THE GULLY (924 623 — Ref Map Sheet 37/16 SE) when his tank was hit and put out of action.

He evacuated his crew and then returned to his tank to use the machine gun on an enemy position to his front although the enemy tank, a PANTHER, which had put his tank out of action, was still in the vicinity. Eventually his machine gun jammed and being unable to repair it he again evacuated the tank. He then helped his crew, some of whom were wounded, to get away to safety under heavy mortar, and machine gun fire. He then again returned to his tank to confirm that his Troop Leader was dead and not in need of any help.

This N. C. O. showed the greatest courage and devotion to duty under the most difficult circumstances.

3 065 119 T p r. R. F o s t e r

At 1100 hrs on 16th July 1944, on the high ground above BOUGY (913 607 — Ref Map Sheet 1/25 00 37/16 SE), Tpr. Foster was acting as co-driver of a tank. He saw his Troop Leader's tank put out of action by an enemy anti-tank gun. He drew the attention of his tank commander to this and said that if the Commander would let him he would get out and fix tow ropes to his Troop Leader's tank to tow it to safety.

This he did under heavy mortar fire and shell fire, showing greatest coolness and devotion to duty throughout.

7 893 530 S g t. E. A. M a c L e a n

Sgt. MacLean is Mechanist Sgt. of 'B' Squadron 107 Regt., R. A. C, and at present acting Recovery Sgt. of that Squadron's Armoured Recovery Vehicle.

On 8th February 1945, during the attack on BRUKK (767 528) and BREEDEWEG (766 524), one of the leading tanks of 'B' Squadron developed mechanical trouble, and on hearing this

85

on the Regimental wireless link, Sgt. MacLean, with complete disregard for his own personal safety, immediately proceeded forward under fire and on foot to the tank carrying the necessary spare parts and tools with him. With fighting going on around him he quickly repaired the tank which was thus enabled to rejoin its Troop and continue fighting.

He then saw that two other tanks of his Squadron had slipped off the side of one of the only two roads along which tank going was at all possible, and were consequently blocking one of the vital routes. He therefore guided the Squadron Recovery tank to the spot and assisetd in recovering these two tanks While the second one was being recovered it struck an anti-tank mine which made the recovery work even more difficult. All this work was done under direct enemy machine gun fire from a bulding approximately 300 yards away, the only protection being a smoke screen which was put down by one of the tanks he was recovering. In addition the whole area was infested by anti-tank and Schumines, one of which exploded during the recovery operations seriously injuring three of the tank crew. In spite of this, Sgt. MacLean coolly carried on with his task and succeeded in clearing the road, thus allowing an A.V.R.E. bridge layer to move forward and breech the anti-tank ditch. However, a Flail tank going forward to clear mines on the far side of the newly laid bridge, was struck by a bazooka fired from the same building which had been shooting at the recovery party. The tank was penetrated and brewed up. Thus the road was again blocked. Unperturbed Sgt. MacLean immediately went forward again with his Recovery tank to pull the Flail tank clear of the road. This he did under covering fire from a supporting Tank Troop.

Sgt. MacLean throughout displayed great courage and initiative and outstanding devotion to duty under fire. But for the untiring efforts of this gallant NCO one of the vital routes into the REICHSWALD would not have been open until very much later that day and valuable time affecting the consolidation of 154 Brigade on its objective would have been lost.

7 656 662 S g t. J. J o l l e y (R.E.M.E.)

Sgt. Jolley is commander of a recovery tank. He has on many occasions displayed outstanding gallantry on the battlefield, when recovering knocked out tanks, with complete disregard of his own personal safety.

In one action a tank received a direct hit on the turret in front of our forward infantry localities, putting it out of action. Sgt. Jolly brought his recovery tank up to the crest of the hill and then in full view of the enemy and under intense mortar and small arms fire, crawled forward pulling with him a long tow rope. He connected this to the damaged tank and returning, sucessfully towing it over the crest and preventing further damage. On another occasion two tanks had beeen damaged by mines and were blocking a vital road holding up the advance. Sgt. Jolley took his recovery tank up the road under heavy shell and mortar fire and successfully pulled the tanks clear of the road. These, together with many similar instances, have shown him to be untiring in his devotion to duty under fire. He is brave and cool and his gallantry has been an outstanding example and inspiration to all ranks in battle in the face of the enemy.

97 781 Sgt. Darke J. R. (R.E.M.E.)

Sgt. Darke has served with 107 Regt., R. A. C., since the Regiment landed on the Continent in July 1944. Throughout the whole campaign he had shown outstanding personal courage and a devotion to duty far above the average.
During an attack on ESQUAY (949 608), Sgt. Darke successfully recovered a damaged tank from a minefield under continuous and heavy mortar fire. He reconnoitred a path on foot for his Armoured Recovery Vehicle, lifting mines where necessary, repaired the tank while still under fire, and towed it out of the minefield.
On the ORNE bridgehead near GRIMBOSQ (960 532) when 107 Regt., R. A. C., suffered heavy casualties from enemy Tiger tanks, Sgt. Darke recovered three damaged tanks under very heavy enemy shell and mortar fire.
Again, during the operation of CLARKEFORCE when several tanks were bogged near STONEBRIDGE (889 125) he coolly carried on his task of recovery in the face of an enemy counter-attack supported by armour and under direct fire from enemy S. Ps. He recovered all the tanks with one exception, which was knocked out by enemy 88 mm fire before it could be driven away.
From 8th Feb—28th Feb 1945, Sgt. Darke was in action with 'A' Squadron 107 Regt., R. A. C., during operation 'VERITABLE'. In the initial attack on the REICHSWALD (774 520) on the 8th February two complete troops of his Squadron were seriously bogged. He went immediately to their assistance although they were still under enemy fire and knowing that the area contained anti-tank and Schumines. He worked untiringly during the evening and night of 8th February and assisted by two other armoured recovery vehicles finally recovered all the bogged tanks.

During the same operation on the night 26/27 February a tank was mined while probingg forward of our own infantry positions south of GOCH (9143). With no Infantry support and under heavy HE fire, Sgt. Darke took his armoured recovery vehicle forward, repaired the track on the spot and brought it back to our own lines.

His recovery work throughout has always been of the same high standard. He has at all times shown the greatest courage being untiring in his devotion to duty calmly carrying out his work of recovery under fire with a complete disregard for his own personal safety.

1 506 357 M/Sgt. Symonds E. W. (REME)

On the 8 Aug 1944, during the battle of the ORNE BRHD a tank of 'B' Squadron 107 Regt., R. A. C., broke a track and ran right off it about 50 yards from the ford crossing of the R. ORNE near GRIMBOSQ (960 532). The particular place was under direct enemy small arms fire from a party of the enemy who had infiltrated into some woods overlooking the river from the far bank. Also at intervals hy concentrations of enemy mortar and shell fire were brought down on the area of the ford and bridge. In spite of this, Sgt. Symonds, while the tank crew remained inside the tank, continued to work in the open without any protection or cover until the track was repaired.

His coolness and complete disregard for his own personal safety was a fine example to all who saw him.

Again on the 20 October 1944, at the commencement of the operation of CLARKEFORCE, several tanks of the Regiment were severely bogged in the area of STONEBRIDGE (889 125) NW of WUESTWEZEL. During the night and the morning of the 21 October, the Regiment continued its advance as an armd spearhead in the direction of NIEUWMOER (764 198) leaving Sgt. Symonds with his A. R. V. and one other A. R. V. to recover the bogged tanks at STONEBRIDGE area made it obvious that the enemy was preparing for a counter attack on the bridge. In spite of this Sgt. Symonds continued with the recovery work and with the assistance of the other A. R. V. from another Sqn of the Regt Pulled out all the bogged tanks. During the period a continual enemy mortar and shell fire was being brought down in the area of the bridge and at the end the position was under direct observation from enemy S. Ps. and one of the tanks which had been recovered was in fact knocked out by enemy 88 mm fire before it could be driven away.

On 3 December 1944, during the attack on BLERICK (8909 E) Sgt. Symonds with his A. R. V. accompanied the leading flail and A. V. R. E. tanks to anti-tank ditch over which a crossing had to be made. One flail tank became ditched but although the area of the anti-tank ditch was being subject to severe shell and mortar fire and was under direct observation by the enemy, Sgt. Symonds dismounted from his A. R. V. and personally directed the recovery work in the open. During the course of this operation Sgt. Symonds recovered 8 Churchill tanks, 3 Flail tanks, and four Kangaroos which had either been bogged or blown up by mines.

During operation "VERITABLE" from Feb 8 to Feb 28, Sgt. Symonds again showed untiring devotion to duty, recovering 12 tanks, two of which had been blown up on minefields which were extensive. He was at all times quite untiring in his recovery work and the actions quoted above are typical of the cool courage shown by this NCO under fire.

3 716 283 W/Sgt. Corker W.

During operation "VERITABLE" and on the 2nd day of the battle in the REICHSWALD (774 520) on 9 February 45, when 107 R. A. C. was supporting Bdes of the 51 HD Div. Sgt. Corker was Tp Sjt of a Tp of 'A' Squadron supporting the 7 Bn Argyls. Just when it was expected that the Tp would be ordered to return to Rear Rally The 2nd Bn Seaforths called for support for a night attack. Although Sgt. Corker's Tk was dangerously low in petrol and ammunition he refused to be left out of battle.

After a long advance in the dark the Tp found themselves out of touch with the Infantry and alone on the objective. Simultaneously, the leading tank was fired on by a Bazooka and immediately afterwards the Tp Ldr's Tank was hit by a second Bazooka. Sgt. Corker at once engaged and neutralised the first. at the same time charging the second and running over it with his tracks. This he did with complete disregard for his own safety ,sitting on top of his tank in spite of considerable small arms fire, in effort to direct the fire of his own guns to the best advantage.

He continued to neutralise the enemy's fire whilst the other two tanks took up more favourable positions, knowing full well that his tank presented an excellent target to any anti-tank weapon which could approach within a few yards of his tank, under cover of darkness with perfect safety.

His action on this occasion was typical of the spirit with which he fought his tank during the whole three weeks in action during of the Siegfried Line. By his time less efforts and constant cheerfulness he did much to maintain the high morale of the Troop.

No praise is too high for this gallant NCO's conduct, not only in this particular operation, but indeed throughout the entire campaign.

3 382 809 W/Cpl Taylor W. (A. C. C.)

Cpl. Taylor has served under attachment to 107 R. A. C. since the Regiment landed in Normandy in July 1944. Throughout the whole campaign he has shown marked ability in organising the Squadron cooking arrangements, often under very difficult conditions, and he has never hesitated to come forward with the ration train to ensure that the fighting troops were satisfied.

As an example of this on the night of October 27th 1944 during the operation of CLARKEFORCE, Cpl. Taylor accompanied the single column up to his Squadron, which was harboured in and around a farm building at OOSTLAAR and within range of enemy mortars and artillery. At dawn on October 28th the Squadron came under heavy fire from mortars and SP. guns which hit the petrol lorry and two half tracked vehicles, all three of which were burnt out. The tanks, one of which had been hit had to be hurriedly withdrawn to cover, leaving Cpl. Taylor and his party on their own. He at once took charge, collected the party together and although he had never driven a half tracked vehicle, he turned the remaining one round, in a very confined space and under heavy shell and mortar fire. By this time the farm building was on fire and on learning that there was a wounded infantry man inside, without hesitation Cpl. Taylor left the vehicle, entered the burning building and rescued the wounded man, carried him back, still under shell fire, to the half tracked vehicle. He then drove the party back to safety.

His courage on this occasion undoubtedly saved the life of the wounded infantry man, and by his quick grasp of the situation he almost certainly saved his own party from suffering casualties, and the last vehicle from being destroyed by enemy shell fire.

The above is an example of this NCO's tireless devotion to duty and entire disregard for his own personal safety, rising to a high standard of courage when the occasion demanded. This together with his constant cheerfulness under all conditions has proved an inspiration to all who have worked with him.

Croix-de Guerre — Bronze Star

3 715 772 L / C. E. Garner

On the night of Monday 7th August 1944, L/Cpl. Garner was the driver in a Churchill tank in 5 Troop of 'A' Squadron 107 Regt., R. A. C. (King's Own) which had been cut off by the enemy.

The crew, with Sgt. Atkinson, had baled out of the tank under orders, and three of the crew, viz. Sgt. Atkinson, L/Cpl. Garner and Tpr. Robinson, were wounded.

L/Cpl. Garner then, despite a shrapnel wound in his thigh found a route down to the River through enemy positions and ordered the remainder of the crew to carry Sgt. Atkinson down to the River bank. L/Cpl. Garner then, with Tpr. Morris, made his way to the bridge, which was dominated by the enemy and found a stretcher, returned to Sgt. Atkinson and brought him and the remainder of the crew back to the bridge. Thus he probably saved the life of his tank commander. L/Cpl. Garner was later evacuated owing to his wound.

Croix-de Guerre 1940 — With Palm (Class 5)

3 708 694 Sgt. Rowlandsohn J.

During Operations from 20 th October 1944 to 29th October 1944, in the advance of an Armd Column from WUESTWEZEL 8216 to WOUW 6630, Sgt, Rowlandsohn, on many occasions showed the utmost daring and determination in dealing with many SP. guns which were endeavouring to hinder the advance. On one particular occasion an SP. had knocked out the Troop Leaders tank of the Troop to which Sgt. Rowlandson was Troop Sgt. He immediately took Command of the remaining two Tanks and by skilfull manoevre knocked out the enemy A. F. V. with his own gun. This meant completely exposing his own Tank to the enemy in order that he may get a shot at it. On another occasion during the same operation, his Troop Leaders Tank was hit by another SP. Gun and in engaging this, Sgt. Rowlandson's Tank was itself hit in the Turret. Sgt. Rowlandsohn, however continued to engage the enemy from his damaged Tank and forced it to withdraw, thus allowing the advance to continue. The operations concerned were designed to free the great Port of Antwerp and resulted in the final liberation of Belgium except for OSTEND.

During the whole of the operations, Sgt. Rowlandson showed the keenest desire to engage the enemy at all times and was an inspiration to those who served with him, his example was largely responsible for the fine spirit in his Troop.

MENTIONS IN DESPATCHES

The following Officers and Other Ranks have been awarded Mentions in Despatches.

Major S. H. P. K. Greenway
Capt. D. J. Phillips MC
Lieut. T. J. Jackson (Killed in Action)
Lieut. S. H. G. Johnstone
Sgt. L. Thorpe
Major P. E. Tapson
Capt. R. E. Webb
Lieut. P. S. Sturgeon
Sgt. E. Brooks
Lieut. F. Boulter
Tpr. J. Morey
Lieut. K. J. Spratt
Capt. J. S. McMartin MC
Lcpl. D. Stickland
Capt. G. F. Griffith
Lieut. D. C. H. Sutherland
Sgt. W. Corker
Sgt. J. L. Rowlandson
Cpl. C. A. Last

C-in-C Certificates

The following Other Ranks have been awarded C-in-C Certificates.

    7 899 455 MQMS Ardley B.
    6 146 043 AQMS Marsden E. J. (REME)
    7 612 781 Cfn. Storey P.
    3 716 339 Sgt. Boote E.
    3 714 039 Tpr. Saunderson G.
    7 951 278 Tpr Ward A.
    7 934 283 Tpr. Scammell J. W.
    5 188 833 Tpr. Smith G. W.
    3 718 209 Tpr. Kinghorn R.
    5 770 863 Pte. Smith B. W. (ACC)
    3 715 712 Tpr Etheridge H.
    3 715 778 Tpr Furby E.
    3 716 358 Tpr. Eckersley H.
    3 716 913 Tpr Wilson G. E.
    3 712 939 Sgt. Woods R.
    7 907 564 MQMS Miller W.

The above list of awards is not final, names of futher personnel have been submitted but not yet authorised.

Milton Keynes UK
Ingram Content Group UK Ltd.
UKHW051644081024
449373UK00019B/293